POLITICS, AMERICAN STYLE

POLITICS,
AMERICAN STYLE

Political Parties in American History

ISOBEL V. MORIN

Twenty-First Century Books
Brookfield, Connecticut

Cover photographs courtesy of Smithsonian Institution, National Museum of American History, Political History Collection and Corbis/Bettman.

Photographs courtesy of Smithsonian Institution, National Museum of American History, Political History Collection: p.3; Corbis-Bettmann: pp. 12, 47; Brown Brothers: p. 19; The Granger Collection, New York: pp. 28, 44, 72, 81, 84, 87, 99, 112; Corbis/Baldwin H. Ward: p. 62; © Stock Mongage: p. 104; Rothco Cartoons: pp. 122 (Renault/Sacramento Bee, CA), 126 (Wicks/The Signal, CA)

Library of Congress Cataloging-in-Publication Data
Morin, Isobel V., 1928–
Politics, American style: political parties in American history/
Isobel V. Morin.
p.   cm.
Includes bibliographical references and index.
ISBN 0–7613–1267–6 (lib. bdg.)
1. Political parties—United States—History.   I. Title.
JK2261.M59   1999
324.273'09—dc21   98–5323   CIP

Published by Twenty-First Century Books
A Division of The Millbrook Press, Inc.
2 Old New Milford Road
Brookfield, Connecticut 06804

CONTENTS

THE EMERGENCE OF THE FIRST POLITICAL PARTIES: THE FEDERALISTS AND ANTI-FEDERALISTS

On September 17, 1787, a group of men gathered at Philadelphia's City Tavern to enjoy a farewell dinner. They had good reason to celebrate. They had completed the first step in a daring political maneuver—the creation of a brand-new American government.

The group had been working on this project for almost four months. Ostensibly gathered for the purpose of revising the Articles of Confederation, under which the thirteen former British colonies had operated since 1781, the delegates at the Philadelphia convention soon began drawing up a new Constitution with greatly increased powers for the central government.

The framers of the Constitution generally shared the dislike of Americans for political parties, which they viewed as selfish factions that sought to promote their own interests without regard to the best interests of society as a whole. These men hoped that the new government would prevent the formation of such factions. However, in tackling the difficult job of getting the country to accept the new Constitution, they acted very much like members of political parties.

Although most people agreed that the Articles needed to be changed, many Americans (including some delegates to the Philadelphia convention) opposed the idea of a strong central government. They were afraid that power once given could never be taken away. Moreover, they feared that those holding political power would tend to increase it, perhaps resulting in the destruction of people's personal liberties.

The secrecy of the proceedings in Philadelphia intensified people's fears. The delegates had agreed to keep their discussions secret to encourage a frank exchange of views, but many citizens viewed the secrecy as evidence of a plot to destroy the individual state governments, perhaps even to establish a monarchy in America. The secrecy gave the supporters of the Constitution one big advantage, however. It gave them a head start in organizing and presenting their arguments to the public.

FEDERALISTS AND ANTI-FEDERALISTS

The new Constitution needed the approval of the Confederation Congress and at least nine states to take effect. To convince the public of the need to approve it, three of its supporters—Alexander Hamilton, John Jay, and James Madison—wrote a series of articles explaining and defending its provisions. They then persuaded sympathetic newspaper editors to publish these articles. The supporters of the Constitution also pulled off a brilliant political maneuver. They called themselves Federalists, and distributed their pro-Constitution articles in a publication titled *The Federalist*. The name implied that the new government would not be a radical departure from the old one. It would still be a federal government, one in which the states would share power with the central government.

The Federalists referred to the opponents of the Constitution as Anti-Federalists. This name suggested that the opponents had no positive ideas of their own but were simply against the new Constitution. This was true to some extent. Those who opposed the Constitution, caught off guard by the presentation of a comprehensive plan for a new government, had to scramble to produce persuasive arguments against it, or even to agree on what aspects of it they disliked. The lack of organization and unity among the Anti-Federalists hurt their efforts to prevent the adoption of the Constitution.

POLITICAL TACTICS AT THE RATIFICATION CONVENTIONS

The Federalists used other political tactics during the ratification conventions to rally support for the Constitution and to stop its opponents from voting it down in conventions where the Anti-Federalists outnumbered them. Moreover, on at least one occasion they employed political tricks to achieve their aim.

One significant political trick took place in Pennsylvania shortly after the Philadelphia convention completed its work. The Federalists had a majority in the state legislature, which was in session at that time. When the Federalists asked the legislature to authorize a ratification convention, the Anti-Federalists tried to block a vote by staying away from the legislative session, thus preventing the attendance of enough members to allow the legislature to conduct business. However, the Federalists had the absent members rounded up and forcibly brought to the legislative chamber. When they had dragged in enough members, the legislature promptly voted for a convention to meet on November 21, 1787, less than two months away.

The Anti-Federalists complained that the short deadline gave people insufficient time to select their delegates and study the provisions of the Constitution. The Federalists ignored these complaints. Pennsylvania ratified the Constitution on December 12, 1787.

When the New Hampshire ratification convention met in February 1788, a majority of the delegates were Anti-Federalists. The Federalists prevented them from voting down the Constitution by persuading the convention to delay further action until June. (The February session had barely enough delegates present to allow it to conduct business, and the Federalists successfully argued that a decision by such a small group would be unfair.) By the time the convention reassembled, the Federalists had convinced a majority of the delegates to vote for ratification. On June 21, 1788, New Hampshire became the ninth state to ratify the Constitution, thus creating a new national government.

This 1788 cartoon shows the states that had ratified the Constitution as pillars supporting the arches of government. The next two pillars, Virginia and New York, would be raised next. With the ninth state, New Hampshire, in place, the Constitution became law.

POLITICAL PROMISES AND THE BILL OF RIGHTS

A common objection to the Constitution was that it lacked a written guarantee of the people's individual rights. The supporters of the Constitution argued that the document itself protected people's rights. Moreover, any listing of rights might imply that the people didn't have any rights that were not on the list. Their arguments were unconvincing, however. In several states the Federalists obtained ratification of the Constitution only after promising to push for a bill of rights as soon as the new Congress met.

THE NEW GOVERNMENT BEGINS ITS OPERATIONS

Federalists dominated the new government, which began operating in March 1789. The newly elected president was George Washington, who had presided over the 1787 convention. Washington's prestige and the enormous respect he commanded did much to ensure that the new government got off to a good start. The Federalists also had a large majority in the new Congress. The presence of so many Federalists in the new central government helped to ensure that its initial structure and important first laws were consistent with the intent of the framers of the Constitution. Perhaps the most important contribution of the First Congress to the establishment of a stable political system was its passage of the ten constitutional amendments known as the Bill of Rights. These amendments became part of the Constitution in December 1791.

POLITICAL SPLITS APPEAR IN THE NEW GOVERNMENT

The hopes of the framers of the Constitution that the officials in the new government would unite to promote the country's best interests soon proved to be false. The problem was that these officials disagreed on how these interests could be served. Splits showed up in Washington's Cabinet as well as in Congress. Alexander Hamilton, the secretary of the treasury, and Thomas Jefferson, the secretary of state, quarreled frequently over political issues. To make matters worse, the two men developed a deep personal animosity toward each other.

One major disagreement between Hamilton and Jefferson concerned Hamilton's proposals for dealing with the government's financial problems. Both the states and the Continental Congress had accumulated huge debts in fighting the Revolutionary War. Although some states had worked hard to repay their debts, massive amounts remained unpaid. As a result, investors were reluctant to extend any further credit to the Americans. The country also was burdened by the generally worthless paper money that the states and Congress had issued during the war.

Hamilton made several proposals to solve these problems. He suggested that the federal government assume responsibility for the payment of the states' debts. He also proposed the imposition of tariffs on certain imported goods to raise money to pay these debts. Finally, Hamilton proposed that Congress establish a national bank to hold the government's money and to provide a dependable currency to replace the worthless paper money issued during past periods.

THE DISPUTE OVER THE BANK OF THE UNITED STATES

Hamilton's proposal for establishment of a national bank was controversial. Many people questioned the authority of Congress to establish it. Hamilton pointed out that the Constitution in Article I, Section 8, gives Congress the authority to make all laws that are necessary and proper to carry out its enumerated responsibilities. In his view this authority included the right to take actions that are implied as part of the responsibilities of Congress even though the Constitution does not specifically mention them.

Jefferson disagreed with Hamilton on this point. Although he had strongly favored the adoption of the Constitution, he believed that its provisions should not be stretched beyond their actual words. Since the Constitution did not specifically give Congress the power to establish a bank, Jefferson believed that Congress did not have this authority.

Surprisingly, Madison agreed with Jefferson on this issue. Madison, who is often called the Father of the Constitution, had vigorously asserted the need for a strong national government during both the 1787 convention and the ratification period. Moreover, in Article 44 of *The Federalist* he had advanced arguments similar to those of Hamilton on the question of the implied powers of Congress. It is not entirely clear why Madison changed his mind when it came to the issue of the national bank. He apparently feared that the bank, which would be controlled by individual investors who could reap large profits from its operations, would widen the gap between the rich and the poor. He may also have suspected that Hamilton really wanted to increase his own power as secretary of the treasury.

These two opposing interpretations of the Constitution regarding the implied powers of Congress have persisted throughout American history. In fact, the debate over the Bank of the United States marked the first clear sign of the emergence of two opposing political parties.

THE FORMATION OF AN OPPOSITION PARTY

By 1796 many of the Anti-Federalists had joined forces with those who believed in a narrow interpretation of the Constitution. Their leader was Jefferson, who left his position in Washington's Cabinet in 1793 to organize an opposition to the Federalists. The members of this group began to call themselves Democratic-Republicans to emphasize their support for the right of ordinary Americans to participate in their government. The name also implied that the Federalists were aristocrats who did not believe in this right. Jefferson's party later shortened its name to Republicans. However, it had no connection with today's Republican party.

DIFFERING VIEWS ON THE ROLE OF THE FEDERAL GOVERNMENT

Jefferson's party disagreed with the Federalists on the role of the federal government. In keeping with his belief in a strict interpretation of the Constitution, Jefferson thought that the federal government should handle only those matters that the individual states could not. He believed, for example, that education and internal improvements such as roads and canals were the responsibility of the states. He also thought that the federal government should tax and spend as little as possible. He particularly objected to the federal government imposing high tariffs on imported goods to protect American businesses from foreign competition. The Federalists, on the other hand, saw nothing wrong with helping American manufacturers by imposing high tariffs on imports, believing that such help would indirectly benefit the entire country.

DIFFERING ATTITUDES TOWARD FRANCE AND ENGLAND

The Federalists and the Jeffersonian Republicans also differed in their attitudes toward France and England. The Republicans generally felt an intense hatred for England dating from the Revolutionary War. They also had warm feelings toward France because of its help in winning American independence. Many Republicans continued to hold France in high regard even after the French Revolution (which most Americans strongly approved at first) deteriorated into an oppressive dictatorship.

The Federalists tended to have more favorable attitudes toward England. The merchants and shipowners of New England, who made up a large percentage of the Federalist party, believed that America's overseas trade (and their own prosperity) depended on peace with England, whose powerful navy controlled the seas. They therefore wanted to maintain friendly relations with that country. Moreover, many Federalists were appalled at the blood-

**This Federalist cartoon shows George Washington
and his federal troops fending off an invasion
by French Republican "cannibals." At right,
Thomas Jefferson and friends try to stop the
"wheels of government," and a dog lifts its
leg on a Republican newspaper.**

bath that occurred in France after radicals took control of the French government. During the so-called Reign of Terror the radicals beheaded King Louis XVI and Queen Marie Antoinette, many other members of the French royalty, and eventually even ardent supporters of the Revolution.

The differing attitudes of the two parties toward France and England, which were complicated by the war between these two countries that broke out in 1793, eventually had fatal consequences for the Federalist party.

WASHINGTON WARNS ABOUT THE "SPIRIT OF PARTY"

Washington deplored the widening split in the new government. In announcing his decision to retire from office at the end of his second term as president, he warned the country about the harmful effects of what he called the "spirit of party," which he believed would weaken the administration of public affairs. In keeping with his dislike of political parties, Washington refused to recommend a successor to his office. He also declined to take an active part in the campaign to choose his successor, leaving this decision in the hands of the two emerging political parties.

THE JEFFERSONIAN REPUBLICANS, THE DEATH OF THE FEDERALIST PARTY, AND THE ERA OF GOOD FEELINGS

In 1796 both the Federalists and the Jeffersonian Republicans worked for the selection of presidential electors who would vote for their candidates. (American presidents are not elected by popular vote, but are chosen by a group of officials called an electoral college.) In a very close election the Federalist candidate, John Adams, was elected president. His political rival, Thomas Jefferson, became vice president. This happened because at that time the Constitution stated that the person who received the highest number of electoral votes (provided they constituted a majority of the total votes) became president, and the person receiving the second-highest number became vice president.

JOHN ADAMS'S VIEWS ON POLITICAL PARTIES

In his inaugural address Adams, who had served as Washington's vice president for eight years, expressed his dismay at the rise of political parties, calling the spirit of party an enemy of the Constitution. Unfortunately for him, the political splits widened during his presidency. His own Federalist party, which held a majority of seats in Congress, disagreed on many issues. Moreover, the members of his Cabinet often disagreed both with him and among themselves on government policies. Adams did his best to mend the splits, but political strife marred his presidency.

Adams, who was never personally popular, failed to win reelection in 1800. He received only sixty-five electoral votes, while Jefferson and the Republican vice-presidential candidate, Aaron Burr, each received seventy-three votes. The House of Representatives eventually broke the tie by selecting Jefferson as president and Burr as vice president.

THE ELECTION OF 1800 PRODUCES A SHIFT OF POLITICAL POWER

The 1800 election resulted in the country's first political realignment—that is, a long-term shift of power from one political party to another. It also showed that a shift of power could be accomplished in a peaceful, orderly fashion instead of by violent revolution, as had occurred often in other countries. The election gave the country not only a Republican president but also a heavily Republican Congress. The Jeffersonian Republicans dominated the federal government throughout the first two decades of the nineteenth century.

One reason for the Republican victory in 1800 was the changing population of the country. When the Constitution was adopted, the population was concentrated along the East Coast. However, the cities also contained a small but growing number of immigrants from other countries, many of whom earned their living by working for others. Also, people were moving away from the coastal areas into the interior of the country. The working-class city residents and the settlers in the rural interior areas generally disliked the Federalists, whom they viewed as too aristocratic to understand the needs of ordinary Americans.

THE REPUBLICANS FORM A POLITICAL ALLIANCE

Another reason for the Republican victory in 1800 was the alliance that Jefferson and his political ally, James Madison, formed during the 1790s among the wealthy southern planters (who tended to dislike the northern commercial leaders), the urban working classes, and the small farmers in the rural interior sections. This diverse group had little in common other than a mutual dislike of the Federalists. That attitude held them together despite their many differences.

Jefferson and Madison strengthened this alliance through newspapers such as the Philadelphia *Aurora,* which supported Republican policies, as well as by personal correspondence. The Federalists, who still controlled Congress and the White House during the 1790s, circulated their own political ideas through the *Gazette of the United States*, a publication supported by generous orders from Hamilton's treasury department for printing government documents.

THE ALIEN AND SEDITION ACTS

In 1798, concerned about the growing number of immigrants, most of whom supported the Republicans, the Federalists in Congress pushed through the Alien and Sedition Acts, which were designed to reduce the power of the Republicans. The three Alien Acts tightened the requirements for obtaining American citizenship (which was generally a requirement for voting) and gave the federal government greater control over aliens (people who are not American citizens), especially during wartime. Although the Federalists claimed that they passed the Alien Acts to lessen the danger of American involvement in the war between France and England that had raged since 1793, many people believed that these laws were enacted mainly to help the Federalists maintain their own political power.

The Sedition Act inflicted much greater harm on the reputation of the Federalists. Angered by the venomous attacks that the Republican newspapers were mounting against the Federalist party and Adams himself, the Federalists in Congress introduced a bill that made the publication of any false or malicious statement about the federal government a crime—that of sedition. (This term refers to any speech or action that causes or advocates discontent or rebellion against the government.) The Sedition Act, which Congress passed in July 1798 by a narrow margin after heated debate, was almost certainly a violation of the First Amendment right to freedom of the press. It was also politically unwise. The arrest and conviction of a few Republican newspaper editors for publishing seditious material, far from silencing the opposition, gave the Republicans a campaign issue in 1800. The Republicans successfully used the Alien and Sedition Acts as evidence that the Federalists were using the powers of the federal government to destroy the personal liberties of the people.

JEFFERSON'S VIEWS ON POLITICAL PARTIES

Jefferson used his own considerable political skills in helping his party to win in 1800. However, like Washington and Adams, Jefferson disliked political parties. In his first inaugural address, after pleading for the restoration of harmony and affection following the election campaign, Jefferson tried to conciliate the defeated Federalists by stating: "Every difference of opinion is not a difference of principle. We have called by different names brethren of the same principle. We are all Republicans—we are all Federalists."[1] Jefferson later stated in a letter to a friend: "The greatest good we can do our country is to heal its party divisions and make them one people."[2] He recognized that new political parties, which seemed to be part of human nature, might arise in the future. He wanted to make sure, however, that the Federalist party, which he despised, would be so discredited that no future party would ever use the name Federalist.[3]

THE WAR OF 1812

In 1802, France and England signed a peace treaty ending the war between the two countries. However, in 1803 the war broke out again, and both France and England resumed their practice of interfering with American merchant ships in an effort to disrupt trade with the enemy.

The war in Europe helped to produce an intensely anti-British Congress in the 1810 election. Many of the anti-British members of Congress, called War Hawks, came from the frontier areas, which were in constant danger of raids by hostile Indian tribes. The frontier settlers, aware that British troops were supporting these tribes, blamed England for the Indian raids. In June 1812 the War Hawks persuaded Congress to declare war on England. Ignoring France's interference with American overseas trade, they justified the war as a response to England's violation of the rights of American sailors and shipowners.

At first the War of 1812 did not go well for the United States. American forces suffered numerous defeats at the hands of the British. In August 1814 the British overran the capital at Washington and burned many government buildings, including the White House, forcing President James Madison and his wife to flee the city. That disaster fueled public opposition to the war, especially in New England, where the wartime disruption of trade had already caused serious economic hardships.

Stop, Stop Stop Brother Jonathan; or I shall fall with the loss of blood— I thought to have been too heavy for you—But I must acknowledge your superior skill—Two blows to my one!—And so well directed too! Mercy mercy on me, how does this happen!!!

Ha—Oh Johnny! you thought yourself a Boxer did you!—I'll let you know we are an Enterprizing Nation. and ready to meet you with equal force any day.

W. Charles del et Sculp

A BOXING MATCH, or Another Bloody Nose for JOHN BULL.

Despite its weak start, the Americans could boast of a few victories early in the War of 1812, including a naval battle between the United States ship *Enterprise* and the British ship *Boxer*. This cartoon uses the names of the ships in a spoof about the battle.

THE HARTFORD CONVENTION AND THE DEATH OF THE FEDERALIST PARTY

In December 1814 a group of New England Federalists met in Hartford, Connecticut, to discuss ways of preventing the recurrence of such disastrous wars.

The convention kept its discussions secret, thus prompting the circulation of rumors that the New England states were planning to secede (or withdraw) from the Union. Some Republicans even accused the convention delegates of plotting treason.

Although some delegates may have wanted New England to secede, the main purpose of the convention was simply to recommend constitutional amendments to decrease the possibility of getting into future wars without the support of the states. However, before the delegates had a chance to present their proposals to Congress, news came of General Andrew Jackson's upset victory over British forces in January 1815 at New Orleans, Louisiana. The resulting surge of nationalist pride and the persistence of rumors of treason by Federalist plotters cost the Federalists what little support they had outside New England.

THE ELECTION OF JAMES MONROE AND THE ERA OF GOOD FEELINGS

In the 1816 presidential election the Republican candidate, James Monroe, who had served as Madison's secretary of state, easily defeated Senator Rufus King of New York, the Federalist candidate. The Federalist party never again named a candidate for president. In 1820, Monroe was reelected by an almost unanimous electoral vote. (The one opposing vote was cast for Monroe's secretary of state, John Quincy Adams.) Meanwhile, the Federalists gradually joined the Republican party, and by the mid-1820s few men called themselves Federalists.

Monroe, like the first four presidents, viewed political parties as divisive elements that tended to destroy the country's political institutions. He once described political parties as "the curse of the country."[4]

Early in Monroe's first term as president a Federalist newspaper, noting the absence of political conflict, described his administration as an "era of good feelings." It remained to be seen whether the country's first taste of one-party government would actually result in political harmony.

A SPLIT IN THE
REPUBLICAN RANKS:
THE ELECTION OF 1824

James Monroe's reelection in 1820 with virtually no opposition seemed to justify the description of his presidency as an Era of Good Feelings. There were signs of trouble to come, however. Although most former Federalists joined the Republican party, they retained their old political views. Moreover, a number of Republicans agreed with the former Federalists on some issues.

In 1816 a Republican Congress approved a charter for the Second Bank of the United States. The

First Bank of the United States had gone out of existence in 1811 after Congress refused to renew its charter. The financial problems resulting from the War of 1812 convinced Congress of the need for a new national bank. In 1816, Congress also enacted a high protective tariff. To old-line Republicans, these new laws signaled a revival of Federalism.

PRESIDENTIAL AMBITIONS DURING MONROE'S ADMINISTRATION

There were also signs of discord in Monroe's Cabinet, which included three men who wanted to succeed him as president. They were Secretary of the Treasury William H. Crawford, Secretary of State John Quincy Adams, and Secretary of War John C. Calhoun. Their ambitions resulted in frequent quarrels during Cabinet meetings.

Monroe also had to contend with two ambitious men who were not members of his Cabinet. One was Henry Clay, who was speaker of the House of Representatives during much of Monroe's presidency. The other rival was Andrew Jackson, the hero of the Battle of New Orleans, who was elected to the U.S. Senate in 1823.

THE MISSOURI COMPROMISE

A more ominous sign of trouble occurred in 1819 when the territory of Missouri applied for admission as a state. Missouri was part of the Louisiana Purchase—the territory that President Jefferson bought from France in 1803. Its constitution permitted slavery. Some northern members of Congress opposed the admission of another slave state because it would upset the balance in the Senate, which was then evenly divided between senators from slave states and those from free states. Congress patched up its disagreement over the admission of Missouri in a compromise that included the admission of Maine in 1820 as a free state, thus opening the door to Missouri's admission the following year. The Missouri Compromise also forbade slavery in those parts of the Louisiana Purchase that lay north of Missouri's southern border (north of the 36 degree, 30 minute line of latitude), but allowed it in areas south of that line.

The battle over the admission of Missouri was the first major split in Congress that was not based on political party lines. The emerging split would eventually align the North against the South over the sensitive issue of slavery—an issue that would arise repeatedly in the future, with disastrous consequences for the country and its political system.

THE ELECTION OF 1824

As his second term drew to a close, Monroe followed the lead of the first four presidents and announced that he would not seek a third term. Monroe also declined to suggest a successor, thus clearing the way for a battle over the presidency.

Since 1796 the Republicans had usually chosen the party's presidential candidate during a meeting of congressional Republicans called a caucus. In 1824 many Republicans questioned whether the party should hold another caucus to choose its candidate. Nevertheless, a small group of Crawford supporters in Congress held a caucus in which they nominated him. Most other congressional Republicans continued to support their own candidates: Adams, Clay, or Jackson. (Calhoun decided to run for vice president after he realized that he couldn't get enough electoral votes to become president.)

By 1824 voting requirements were much less restrictive than they had been when the Constitution was adopted. The newly admitted states had few voting restrictions, and many of the original states had dropped such requirements as property ownership, allowing almost all white male citizens to vote. Also, three-quarters of the states used some form of popular voting to choose presidential electors. In the 1824 election Jackson received the largest number of both popular and electoral votes, although less than a majority. In the electoral vote count Adams came in second, Crawford third, and Clay fourth. Since no one received a majority of the electoral votes, the House of Representatives had to choose the president for the second time in American history.

The Constitution provides that in such a case the House must choose among those who receive the three highest numbers of electoral votes. This meant that Clay, who had hoped that the election would take place in the House, where he had a good chance of winning, was not among those the House could select. At that point Clay, who distrusted Jackson, threw his support to Adams. When the House voted on February 9, 1825, Adams came in first, Crawford (seriously ill after suffering a stroke) came in second, and Jackson finished third.

JOHN QUINCY ADAMS AND THE "CORRUPT BARGAIN"

Jackson and his supporters, angry over Jackson's third-place finish, assumed that his opponents had stolen the election from him. After Adams selected Clay as his secretary of state (an office widely regarded as a steppingstone to the presidency), there were rumors that the selection was the result of a "corrupt bargain" under which Adams promised to give Clay the appointment in exchange for Clay's support in the election. These rumors weakened Adams's ability to govern and may have kept Clay from ever becoming president.

In his first annual message to Congress, Adams asked for the enactment of a sweeping program that included the financing of a national university, an astronomical observatory, scientific exploration, and internal improvements such as roads, canals, and bridges. In calling for internal improvements Adams used arguments strikingly similar to those that Alexander Hamilton had used more than thirty years earlier in making his proposals to the First Congress. Were Adams's proposals those of a true Jeffersonian Republican, or was John Quincy Adams, a former Federalist and the son of a Federalist president, really still a Federalist in disguise? Many Americans thought so.

Subsequent events didn't do much to shake the popular image of John Quincy Adams as the last surviving Federalist. The last straw for many was the enactment in 1828 of a high protective tariff (often called the Tariff of Abominations) loaded with so many special provisions that it satisfied no one.

Now the Republican party seemed to be on the verge of complete disintegration. The Adams-Clay faction began to call themselves National Republicans, while some of Jackson's supporters adopted the name of Democratic-Republicans. The Jackson supporters later shortened their name to Democrats. By the 1828 election this group had organized into a new political party. The man largely responsible for its birth was a New York politician named Martin Van Buren. He believed that political parties, far from being a curse on the country as Monroe had thought, could be a blessing in the hands of the right leaders.

CHAPTER 4

THE FORMATION OF
THE DEMOCRATIC
AND WHIG PARTIES

After John Quincy Adams became president, Martin Van Buren, who was then in the U.S. Senate, opposed what he regarded as the Federalist policies of the president and his secretary of state, Henry Clay. Van Buren believed that the only effective way to block the Adams-Clay policies was to form an opposition party. Van Buren, who had supported William Crawford for president in 1824, switched his support to Jackson because he believed that the popular military hero was the only person capable of defeating the Adams-Clay group in 1828.

Van Buren, who was often called the "Little Magician" by supporters or the "Red Fox" by foes, had acquired considerable political skills as the leader of a group of New York politicians known as the Albany Regency. He now decided to use these skills to gain control of the national government. His efforts to restore Jefferson's principles to the country played a large part in the development of the Democratic party, the first modern American political party.

VAN BUREN'S VIEWS ON POLITICAL PARTIES

Van Buren shared Jefferson's belief that the people could best preserve their individual liberties by maintaining strong state governments and a national government that exercised only those powers the Constitution specifically gave it. He disagreed, however, with Jefferson's opposition to political parties. Van Buren saw parties as a legitimate means for providing the voters with opposing views on political issues. The competition between two parties could also curb the tendency of those holding political power to become tyrannical or corrupt. Van Buren also saw a practical advantage in the existence of political parties. After winning an election, a party could reward loyal members with public offices. By giving people an incentive for supporting the party's policies, a political party could maintain greater control over its members.

Van Buren argued that the revival of the old alliance between the planters of the South and the ordinary people of the North and the western frontier, based on the Jeffersonian principle of a limited role for the federal government, could be used to form a new political party to oppose the Federalist policies of the Adams-Clay group. The existence of two national parties based on these opposing views on the role of the federal government could help to keep sectional disagreements such as the emerging North-South split over slavery from dominating national politics.

THE FORMATION OF THE DEMOCRATIC PARTY

One of Van Buren's first steps in forming a new party was to restore this old alliance. In December 1826, Van Buren and Adams's vice president, John C. Calhoun, agreed to join forces in support of Jackson's election in 1828. Still hoping to become president someday, Calhoun had decided that his best chance was to support Jackson, who seemed likely to become the next president.

Van Buren tried to form a strong party organization like the one he had built in New York. He therefore worked to establish and strengthen state and local party committees, which could nominate candidates for public office and drum up popular support for its nominees. Van Buren also helped to start several party newspapers with the financial backing of Jackson and his supporters in Tennessee.

Jackson directed all of these activities from his home in Nashville. He was too shrewd to disregard the prevailing belief that people shouldn't actively seek the presidency. However, like many other politicians at that time, he saw nothing wrong with working privately to achieve his goal of winning the presidency in 1828.

Meanwhile, the Adams-Clay supporters tried to keep pace with the Democrats in building a political organization. Although they were hampered by the Democrats' persistent accusations of a corrupt bargain between Adams and Clay in 1824, their biggest problem was Adams himself. The president still clung to the old Federalist belief in a government run by wise and virtuous men who did not seek public office. He therefore steadfastly refused to help himself by the use of political patronage. Political patronage—the practice of handing out government jobs to party supporters—had existed since Jefferson's presidency. Adams insisted, however, that appointments to public office should be based on an individual's merit instead of his party membership. As a result, he often refused to remove men from appointive office even after it became clear that they were trying to undermine his administration.

THE ELECTION OF 1828

In 1828, Adams learned that personal integrity and a desire to serve the country's best interests weren't enough to win reelection. In that year's election the attractive, popular Jackson swamped him. Calhoun, who had deserted Adams in 1826, became Jackson's vice president.

Jackson didn't share Adams's views on the use of political patronage. Soon after taking office, he began to remove National Republicans from office and replace them with loyal Democrats. He also used his veto power much more often than previous presidents had done. (When a president vetoes a bill—the term veto comes from the Latin word meaning "I forbid"—it does not become law unless two-thirds of the members of both houses of Congress pass it again. The passage of a law over a president's veto is called an override.) Most presidential vetoes in the past had reflected the president's belief that a law was unconstitutional or that it would have harmful effects. Some of Jackson's vetoes reflected his personal dislike of a bill or his belief that it would give power to his political opponents.

JACKSON'S BANK VETO

One of Jackson's most controversial vetoes was his 1832 veto of a bill to extend the charter of the Second Bank of the United States, which was due to expire in 1836. (Congress had established this bank in 1816.) Jackson had long opposed this bank as an unconstitutional abuse of congressional authority. He also believed that the bank, which was controlled by a small group of directors who profited financially from its operations, gave too much power to a few individuals. Many people supported the bank, however, because they believed that a national bank was essential to the maintenance of a uniform and stable system for the circulation of money.

Jackson's veto of the bank bill gave Henry Clay what he thought was a winning issue in the 1832 presidential election campaign. Clay thought that a majority of voters would agree with him on the need for a national bank. Jackson's arguments against the bank were persuasive to many voters, however. Jackson, a popular war hero, easily defeated Clay, the National Republicans' candidate, for a second term as president.

OPPOSITION TO JACKSON DEVELOPS

Despite Jackson's enormous popularity with ordinary Americans, many thought he was too likely to exceed his constitutional authority in an attempt to enlarge his own personal power. For example, Jackson in

Andrew Jackson (left) is shown battling a serpent with many heads in this cartoon. The heads represent the states as well as issues and opponents that Jackson was up against in his presidency. The sword he uses is labeled "veto."

1833 ordered the removal of government deposits from the Second Bank of the United States. He then deposited the funds in several state banks. (Jackson's opponents called these "pet banks" because the president's supporters controlled them.) Many members of Congress, including Clay, believed that Jackson had exceeded his authority in transferring the money without the approval of Congress.

THE SOUTH CAROLINA NULLIFICATION CRISIS

Jackson also angered many South Carolina residents by his actions during a dispute over tariffs. Southerners, who depended on imports for many manufactured products, generally opposed high tariffs because they increased the price of these goods. In November 1832 the South Carolina legislature nullified tariffs that Congress had imposed in 1828 and 1832. (Nullification means a declaration that a certain act has no effect.) The legislature, after declaring that the tariffs were unconstitutional, warned that any use of force to compel the payment of these taxes would be grounds for the state's secession from the Union. Jackson, although he generally supported states' rights, also believed that the states had no authority either to refuse to obey a federal law or to secede from the Union. He therefore persuaded Congress to give him the authority to use military force if necessary to compel South Carolina to obey the tariff laws. The threatened crisis was averted in 1833 when Congress passed a compromise tariff that Clay drafted. Clay persuaded Calhoun, who was then in the Senate representing South Carolina (he had resigned as Jackson's vice president during the nullification crisis), to support the bill as a way of avoiding the civil war that threatened to break out if Jackson used military force to collect the 1832 tariff.

THE FORMATION OF THE WHIG PARTY

During Jackson's second term his opponents united to form a new political party. The party contained several diverse groups with different and sometimes conflicting interests. It included those who agreed with Clay's support for the national bank, federal financing of internal improvements such as roads and canals, and the use of tariffs to encourage the development of American industry. It also included southern states' rights advocates and some who simply disliked Jackson. The new political party took the name Whigs to remind people of the American patriots during the Revolutionary War who also called themselves Whigs. The Whigs of the 1830s were determined to resist what they called the tyranny of "King Andrew."

BORN TO COMMAND.

OF VETO MEMORY.

HAD I BEEN CONSULTED.

VETO.

CONSTITUTION
of the
UNITED STATES
of America.

Internal Improvements
U.S. Bank

KING ANDREW THE FIRST.

This cartoon makes it very clear what Jackson's opponents thought of him. "King Andrew" stands on a shredded document called "Internal Improvements—U.S. Bank," as well as the torn-up Constitution.

The newly organized Whig party failed to agree on a presidential candidate in 1836. As a result, there were three Whig candidates in the 1836 election: General William Henry Harrison of Ohio, Senator Hugh L. White of Tennessee, and Senator Daniel Webster of Massachusetts. Meanwhile, the Democrats nominated Martin Van Buren, Jackson's choice to succeed him. Although Van Buren received only slightly more than half of the popular votes, he received 170 of the 294 electoral votes, while the deeply divided Whigs managed a combined total of only 113 votes for their three candidates. The South Carolina electors cast all of their 11 votes for a southern "favorite son," Willie P. Mangum of North Carolina.

PARTY CONVENTIONS, PARTY PLATFORMS, AND POLITICAL CARTOONS

During the 1830s the emergence of two new political parties—the Democrats and the Whigs—brought changes in the political landscape. The old method of nominating a party's presidential candidates in a party caucus was replaced by the use of a national convention to select a party's candidate. The first such convention was held in September 1831, when a small political party called the Anti-Masonic party held a national convention during which it nominated a candidate for president. The party soon disappeared from the political scene, but the idea of a nominating convention eventually became the standard method for choosing a party's presidential candidate.

In December 1831 the National Republicans held a convention in which they nominated Clay for president. The Democrats used national conventions to nominate their candidates for president beginning with the 1832 elections. The Whigs held their first national convention in December 1839.

About this time the political parties adopted the practice of drawing up a statement of the party's principles and positions on issues for use in the campaign. The statement of principles was called a platform, and the statements on particular issues were called planks. The platforms and planks often contained ambiguous statements to allow local party organizations to adapt them to local politics.

Political cartoons also became popular during Jackson's presidency. These drawings, which appeared in popular magazines, contained amusing and sometimes sarcastic descriptions of prominent political figures, including Jackson himself.

THE ELECTION OF 1840

By 1840 the Whigs had learned how to get a president elected. First, they realized that they had to unite behind a single candidate. Second, they must pick the candidate with the best chance of winning the election. In December 1839 the Whigs by-passed such prominent party members as Henry Clay and Daniel Webster to nominate William Henry Harrison. As territorial governor of Indiana he had achieved military fame in 1811 by defeating the Shawnee Indians at Tippecanoe Creek. Harrison had also made the best showing of the three Whig candidates in the 1836 election, receiving 73 of the 113 electoral votes cast for Whigs.

The convention also nominated John Tyler for vice president. A former Democrat from Virginia who had broken with his party over the removal of government money from the Second Bank of the United States, Tyler was chosen to give the party both geographic and political balance.

The Whigs also copied the Democrats' campaign tactics in 1840. To appeal to ordinary Americans, who tended to vote Democratic, they held parades and rallies during which they portrayed Harrison as a common person who lived in a log cabin. (Harrison, who came from a prominent Virginia family, actually lived in a comfortable house in Ohio.) They even published a party newspaper called the *Log Cabin*, and adopted a campaign slogan, "Tippecanoe and Tyler, Too." In 1840 the Whigs also enlisted campaign workers to go around seeking support for Harrison (a practice called canvassing). Aided by a deep economic depression that began early in Van Buren's presidency and by the president's lack of personal charm, the Whigs easily defeated him in 1840. The Whigs also won a majority of seats in Congress and the state legislatures.

JOHN TYLER'S PRESIDENCY

The Whigs were unlucky in their choice of candidates, however. President Harrison died of pneumonia only a month after taking office, making Tyler president. The choice of Tyler for vice president proved to be a monumental error for the Whigs. Although he had joined the Whig party, Tyler hadn't changed his Democratic belief in states' rights and a narrow interpretation of the powers of Congress under the Constitution. He vetoed several important Whig bills, which the Whigs were unable to override. A group of congressional Whigs, frustrated by Tyler's actions, then voted to expel him from the party.

The Whigs' frustrations continued after the 1842 elections, in which the Democrats won a majority of nearly two to one in the House. Although the Whigs narrowly kept control of the Senate, the divisions in the federal government prevented the Whigs from accomplishing much during the remainder of Tyler's term.

Congress made two significant changes that affected future elections, however. One change involved the method of electing members of the House of Representatives. Under the old system the states that were entitled to more than one House member could decide whether to divide the state into two or more congressional election districts, each of which would elect one House member, or elect all of their House members on an "at large" or statewide basis. The "at large" elections used by some states enabled one party to elect all of the state's House members even though another party had a majority of voters in certain parts of the state. The new law required the state legislatures to draw up single-member election districts, thus giving local voters a chance to elect someone from their own political party even though another party held a majority in the state as a whole.

The second change set a uniform date for holding national elections. Previously, the states had held national elections on different days. The new law specified that national elections were to be held on the Tuesday following the first Monday in November, a date that can fall anywhere between November 2 and November 8. Both changes are still in effect.

Although Congress and President Tyler deadlocked on most political issues, during the closing days of his administration the president set the stage for an act that he hoped would result in the achievement of one of his most cherished goals—his election to a full term as president. That act was the annexation of the Republic of Texas as part of the United States.

THE DEATH OF THE WHIG
PARTY AND THE FORMATION
OF THE REPUBLICAN PARTY

In 1836 a group of American settlers in Texas had succeeded in winning independence from Mexico. These Texans then asked to become part of the United States. The leaders of both the Democratic and Whig parties tried to avoid any discussion of the annexation of Texas, fearing that this would divide their parties by reviving the question of the expansion of slavery into new territories, which the Missouri Compromise had apparently settled. President Tyler, who had become a "president without a party" after his expulsion from the Whig party, wasn't concerned about such divisions. He hoped that by bringing Texas into the Union he could establish a new political party, which would nominate him for president in 1844. He also firmly believed, along with many Americans at that time, that the United States was destined to expand across much, if not all, of North America.

In April 1844, Tyler sent the Senate a proposed treaty with Texas under which that republic agreed to be annexed by the United States. The Senate rejected the treaty in June. Tyler then sent the treaty to the House of Representatives for consideration as a joint resolution under which a majority of both houses of Congress would agree to annex Texas. In late February 1845, Congress passed a joint resolution offering statehood to Texas. On March 3, 1845, Tyler, in one of his last acts as president, invited Texas to join the Union as a state.

The annexation of Texas was a significant issue during the 1844 presidential election campaign. Most Whigs and some Democrats opposed it because they were afraid that the addition of the new territory would revive the question of the expansion of slavery. Many southern Democrats, on the other hand, favored annexation because it could increase the number of slave states.

The Democratic candidate, James K. Polk, a strong advocate of annexation, defeated the Whig candidate, Henry Clay, who was making his third and last run for the presidency. The popular vote was close, however. Polk's victory depended on New York's electoral votes, which he won by a margin of not much more than 5,000 votes.

THE MEXICAN WAR

In January 1846, Congress formally admitted Texas as a state. Shortly after, Polk ordered American troops under the command of General Zachary Taylor to patrol the area near the Rio Grande, which Mexico claimed as part of its territory. In May, after Mexican troops attacked an American scouting party, Congress declared war on Mexico. The war quickly ended in an American victory, giving the United States a huge expanse of new territory, called the Mexican Cession, that ran all the way to the Pacific Ocean. The acquisition of this territory, which included the present states of Utah, Nevada, and California, as well as parts of Arizona, New Mexico, Colorado, and Wyoming, proved to be a mixed blessing. The ensuing controversy over the issue of slavery in the new territory pitted the North against the South in an increasingly hostile debate that eventually threatened the continued existence of the Union itself.

The issue flared up even before the end of the war. In August 1846, while the House was considering a bill to provide money for the army, a Pennsylvania Democrat named David Wilmot introduced an amendment that would have forbidden slavery in any territory acquired as a result of the war. Congress never enacted this provision, which became known as the Wilmot Proviso, but it served to harden attitudes in both the North and the South on the issue of slavery in the territories.

THE ELECTION OF 1848

The 1848 treaty with Mexico, which resulted in the Mexican Cession, made Wilmot's proposal an immediate practical issue. In an emotionally charged atmosphere, both parties struggled to keep the issue from dividing the country along sectional lines during the 1848 presidential election.

The Democratic candidate, Lewis Cass of Michigan, tried to bypass the issue by suggesting that the residents of the new territory be allowed to decide for themselves whether to permit slavery. This angered some northern Democrats who opposed any further expansion of slavery. These Democrats joined some northern Whigs to form a new political party, the Free-Soil party, which named former president Martin Van Buren as its presidential candidate.

The Whigs nominated the popular Mexican war hero, Zachary Taylor, as their candidate. Taylor, a southern slaveowner, described himself as a "no party" candidate who could end party divisions and unite the country under his leadership. Because Taylor didn't state his views on the issue of slavery in the new territory, he had supporters in both the North and the South. Southerners believed they could trust a fellow southerner to support the South on this issue, while northern Whigs pointed out that if a Whig majority in Congress passed some version of the Wilmot Proviso, Taylor would stick to his campaign promise not to veto congressional legislation unless it clearly violated the Constitution.

Taylor's popularity and his refusal to give clear statements of his views on the slavery question helped him to win the 1848 election. However, the Democrats won a majority of seats in Congress. Moreover, many Whigs distrusted Taylor because they didn't believe he was a true Whig. These factors did not favor a successful presidency for the former war hero.

THE DISPUTE OVER THE ADMISSION OF CALIFORNIA

In late January 1850, Senator Henry Clay (one of the Whig leaders in Congress) presented a comprehensive plan for resolving the problems associated with the acquisition of the Mexican Cession. One element of Clay's plan called for the admission of California (whose population had expanded enormously following the discovery of gold in the Sacramento Valley in 1848) as a state without any mention of slavery, leaving its residents free to decide for themselves whether to allow it. On February 13, 1850, while Congress was considering Clay's plan, President Taylor sent Congress a copy of California's constitution and its formal request for admission to the Union as a state. Since California's constitution prohibited slavery, its admission as a free state would disrupt the balance between slave and free states, which then stood at fifteen each. The debate over the admission of California, which included the entire question of slavery in the Mexican Cession, divided Congress along sectional as well as party lines.

The debate over the Mexican Cession also exposed the deep split within the Whig party over this issue. In May 1850, after President Taylor had made public his opposition to Clay's proposals, Clay responded with a series of speeches charging that the president's policy would lead to disunion.

Meanwhile, John C. Calhoun, who had been trying for some time to organize a Southern Rights party, made one last attempt to do so. In January 1849, Calhoun called for the uniting of all southerners in the defense of slavery against what he termed northern aggression. Democrats in a number of southern states responded by calling for a convention to meet in Nashville, Tennessee, in June 1850 to decide on ways to resist the perceived aggression. The Nashville Convention, which drew delegates (mainly Democrats) from nine southern states, condemned Clay's compromise proposals, and agreed to meet again in September to consider further action. The possibility of a breakup of the Union, which had always hung over the country, now threatened to become a reality.

As the crisis mounted, an unexpected event occurred. The president died on July 9, 1850, after a brief illness, making Vice President Millard Fillmore the new president. Shortly after Taylor's death, Congress passed several separate bills that incorporated most of Clay's proposals. Fillmore, who supported these measures, signed them into law.

THE COMPROMISE OF 1850

The Compromise of 1850, as the bills were known collectively, contained several different provisions. One admitted California as a free state, while another provided for the organization of territorial governments in both New Mexico and Utah, leaving them free to decide for themselves whether to allow slavery. The Compromise also enacted a tough new fugitive slave law dealing with the return of escaped slaves to their owners, but tried to sweeten the deal by ending the slave trade in the District of Columbia.

At the second session of the Nashville Convention in September 1850, its delegates rejected the Compromise and called for secession. Nothing much came of these threats, however, because southerners soon began to rally in support of the Compromise.

Although the Compromise of 1850 temporarily settled the slavery question, it seriously damaged the Whig party. The Whigs were not only deeply divided on the Compromise, but its passage also deprived them of the most important national issue that separated them from the Democrats. At the same time two local issues—temperance (or opposition to the use of alcoholic beverages) and nativism (or anti-immigrant bias)—gained prominence, resulting in the formation of a third political party, the Know-Nothing party.

THE RISE OF THE KNOW-NOTHING PARTY

During the 1840s and 1850s large numbers of immigrants thronged to the United States. The newcomers, who came mainly from Ireland and Germany, brought with them customs and beliefs that differed from those of native-born Americans. Many of them were Roman Catholics, whose religious beliefs and ceremonies seemed superstitious to American Protestants. The church's hierarchical (or top-down) structure, headed by the pope in Rome, also seemed to conflict with the American ideals of equality and independence. Moreover, the immigrants often drank alcoholic beverages, which many Americans regarded as a source of social ills. These people often blamed the Irish and German immigrants for the problems related to excessive drinking.

The Know-Nothing movement combined the issues of temperance and nativism with a desire to reform the political system. During the early 1850s many Americans saw little to choose between the Democrats and the Whigs, which seemed to have deteriorated into corrupt organizations filled with unprincipled politicians who sought only their own personal gain. The party bosses in the large cities, where many immigrants settled, often used bribery, coercion, and voting fraud to swell the vote total for the party's candidates. This behavior reinforced the negative image of political parties.

Spurred by these concerns, the Know-Nothing movement grew rapidly, spreading into a number of states in both the North and South. At first the organization operated as a secret society, with passwords, secret handshakes, and the like. In 1855 it publicly entered politics under the name of the American party. By that time the Whig party was in serious trouble.

**The Know-Nothings charged that Irish and
German immigrants were stealing American
elections and running the big-city political machines.
This derogatory cartoon shows the two, dressed
in barrels of Irish whiskey and German beer,
running off with an election ballot box.**

THE ELECTION OF 1852

In the election of 1852 there were few issues on which
the Democrats and Whigs differed. After a half-
hearted campaign, the Democrat, Franklin Pierce,
defeated the Whig candidate, General Winfield Scott.

Although Pierce's margin in the popular vote was fairly small, his electoral vote total greatly outnumbered Scott's. Moreover, the Democrats won majorities in both houses of Congress. The defeat demoralized the Whigs, who were already mourning the deaths of two of their most prominent members—Henry Clay and Daniel Webster. The party never recovered from the 1852 defeat. Although it remained in existence for several years at state and local levels, it never again nominated a presidential candidate.

THE KANSAS-NEBRASKA CONTROVERSY

For a time it appeared that the American, or Know-Nothing, party would replace the Whig party as the major alternative to the Democrats. However, Congress in 1854 passed a law that brought the issue of the expansion of slavery back to national prominence. The law was the Kansas-Nebraska Act, which authorized the formation of governments in the Kansas and Nebraska territories. The act gave these governments the authority to decide whether to allow slavery, even though the Missouri Compromise of 1820 prohibited slavery in these areas (which were part of the Louisiana Purchase) because they lay north of Missouri's southern border. Many northerners were outraged over this law, which they regarded as a blatant attempt by the South to force slavery on the rest of the country. The surge of northern outrage resulted in the formation of a coalition of opponents of the Kansas-Nebraska Act. This loose coalition quickly developed into a new political party, the Republican party.

THE EMERGENCE OF THE REPUBLICAN PARTY

The Republican party's primary goal was to prevent slavery from spreading into any new territories. This goal drew the support of Free Soilers as well as northern antislavery Democrats and Whigs. The Republicans also successfully used the issues of temperance, nativism, and anti-Catholicism to absorb many of the politically inexperienced Know-Nothings into the party.

In 1856 the Republican party held its first national convention. Its presidential candidate was John C. Frémont, a well-known explorer of the West who was called "The Pathfinder." The American, or Know-Nothing, party nominated former president Millard Fillmore. The Democrats nominated James Buchanan of Pennsylvania, who served as the American minister to England under President Pierce.

Although he was a northerner, Buchanan generally sympathized with the South's position regarding slavery. He condemned the Wilmot Proviso and joined most southern Democrats in supporting the Compromise of 1850. Buchanan easily won the election. The Know-Nothing party, which disappeared from the political scene shortly afterward, won only Maryland's 8 electoral votes. However, Frémont picked up 114 electoral votes. Encouraged by this showing, the Republicans planned to try again in 1860.

There were signs of trouble ahead for the Union, however. The election results showed how deep the sectional split, which had existed for some time, had become. The Democrats had adopted an increasingly proslavery stance because of a rule adopted by the Democratic National Convention in 1832. The rule, which remained in effect until 1936, required that a candidate receive the votes of at least two-thirds of the convention delegates to win the Democratic nomination for president. This rule ensured that the Democrats would not nominate anyone who was not acceptable to the South—in other words, anyone who did not support the southern Democrats' position regarding slavery.

In the 1856 presidential election the Republicans won in most of the free states, but the Democrats captured almost all of the slave states.

POLITICAL PARTIES
DURING THE CIVIL WAR

In 1860 the Republicans nominated Abraham Lincoln, a comparatively unknown former Whig from Illinois, for president. The Democrats, who were unable to agree on a candidate, split into two factions. The southern faction nominated President Buchanan's vice president, John C. Breckinridge of Kentucky. The northern faction nominated Senator Stephen A. Douglas of Illinois. A third group of former Whigs and Know-Nothings formed the Constitutional Union party, with John C. Bell of Tennessee as its candidate.

Lincoln won in almost every northern state, giving him a majority of the electoral votes. The election of

Lincoln, the candidate of a sectional party whose platform was based on antislavery with virtually no southern support, prompted seven southern states to secede from the Union shortly after. Four other states followed, making a total of eleven states to leave the Union.

While both Republicans and Democrats in Congress scrambled to find ways of resolving the crisis, Lincoln worked on the formation of his Cabinet. Recognizing both the danger of the complete collapse of the Union and the fragility of the Republican coalition, Lincoln picked Cabinet members with an eye toward diversity of political views as well as sectional balance. His choices included two of his strongest Republican rivals: William H. Seward for secretary of state and Salmon P. Chase for secretary of the treasury. Lincoln also asked several southerners to join his Cabinet. All of them refused, but two men from the border states of Maryland and Missouri agreed to accept Cabinet posts. His final Cabinet selections included four former Democrats and three former Whigs.

This diverse group of men, some of whom had presidential ambitions, often disagreed on political issues. Some of them developed personal animosities toward each other. It took great personal and political skills to smooth over these differences while maintaining control over important decisions. Fortunately, Lincoln had an abundance of both skills.

POLITICAL PATRONAGE UNDER LINCOLN

Lincoln also understood the value of political patronage in building and maintaining support for his party. After taking office, he removed most Democrats from appointive offices and replaced them with Republicans. The selection of replacements was a tedious and difficult process in which Lincoln often had to consider the sensitivities of Republican leaders in the various states as well as an individual's personal qualifications for a job. Here again Lincoln put his skills to good use.

POLITICS IN THE CONFEDERACY

Meanwhile, the seceding states were forming their own government. The leaders of the new Confederate States of America hoped to return to a form of government in which political parties would disappear and the voters would choose only good and wise men for public office. However, just as the Jeffersonian Republicans had discovered during James Monroe's presidency, the Confederates learned that a government without political parties tends to split into factions regardless. These factions often are based on personal ambitions and animosities rather than differences of opinion on political issues. The Confederate factions, which too often kept the southern leaders from putting aside their personal differences and uniting to achieve their goal of independence, did much to bring about the eventual defeat of the South in the Civil War.

THE EFFECT OF SECESSION ON CONGRESS

The secession of eleven southern states had a dramatic effect on the composition of the incoming Congress in 1861. After these states seceded, all of their House members and twenty-one of their twenty-two U.S. senators resigned from their offices. (Only Senator Andrew Johnson of Tennessee, who believed that the states had no right to secede, remained in Congress.) Since most of the members of Congress who resigned were Democrats, their departure left both the House and the Senate with large Republican majorities. This gave the Republicans the opportunity to pass many bills that the Democrats had blocked because of their belief in limited government. Among these bills were a new protective tariff, federal aid for the building of transcontinental railroads, and grants of federally owned land for agricultural colleges and for the settlement of the West.

REPUBLICANS IN CONGRESS

Confederate forces attacked and captured Fort Sumter in Charleston, South Carolina, in April 1861, beginning the Civil War. Most northerners agreed that the government had to use force to put down the rebellion. Republicans later split on the issue of how vigorously the North should conduct the war and whether its aim should be to end slavery as well as to preserve the Union. One group of dedicated opponents of slavery, called Radicals, insisted that the abolition of slavery was a legitimate war aim. Moderate and conservative Republicans preferred a cautious approach to this controversial issue. They were aware that many northerners saw nothing wrong with slavery. Moreover, the moderate and conservative Republicans were not sure that Congress had the constitutional authority to free the slaves. Although the Radicals tended to be a noisy bunch who caused Lincoln a great deal of trouble, they were never really in control of Congress.

DEMOCRATS IN CONGRESS

The Democrats, who made up such a small minority in Congress, were generally more united than the Republicans on political issues. They divided into two factions regarding the war, however. One faction, called War Democrats, supported the Union's war effort despite the poor performance of the northern armies during the early part of the war. The other faction, called Peace Democrats, wanted an end to the bloody and costly war even if it meant recognizing the independence of the Confederacy. This stance led many Republicans to accuse the Peace Democrats of disloyalty. They used the term "Copperheads" to describe the Peace Democrats, comparing them to poisonous copperhead snakes.

Undoubtedly, some Peace Democrats deserved that name. Sympathy for the South and in some cases outright disloyalty to the Union were widespread in parts of the North. This was especially true in the Midwest and in the areas near the Confederate border, where pro-Confederate secret societies encouraged disloyal activities. For the most part, however, the Peace Democrats remained loyal to the Union even though they disagreed with many of the government's policies regarding the war.

EMANCIPATION BECOMES A WAR AIM

Although Lincoln shared the concerns of moderate and conservative Republicans about the wisdom of emancipating (or freeing) the slaves, by the summer of 1862 he had decided that this action was neces-

Lincoln's aim of freeing the slaves was met with widespread cynicism, as this 1862 British cartoon shows. Lincoln is shown as a cunning figure persuading a former slave to join the Union forces as a favor for freeing the man.

sary to save the Union. He reasoned that freeing the slaves would deprive the Confederacy of this valuable human resource and also allow the Union to enlist the former slaves in its war effort. In September 1862 he warned the South that unless it surrendered by the end of the year he would free the slaves in all areas still under Confederate control.

Lincoln's proclamation drew the condemnation of the Democrats, most of whom believed that the federal government did not have the constitutional authority to free the slaves. Lincoln, along with many Republicans in Congress, shared this belief, but he relied on his authority as commander in chief of the armed forces to free the slaves as a temporary war measure.

The Democrats stressed their opposition to emancipation during the congressional election campaigns of 1862. This strategy enabled them to increase their membership in Congress, although the Republicans kept control of that body. The Democrats also won control of three midwestern state legislatures, increased their membership in three others, and elected governors in New York and New Jersey.

THE EMANCIPATION PROCLAMATION

Despite the Republican losses in the elections of 1862, Lincoln fulfilled his promise to free the slaves. On January 1, 1863, he issued the Emancipation Proclamation, which declared that the slaves in all areas under Confederate control were free. Lincoln's action was largely symbolic. It is doubtful whether it actually freed any slaves. It did have one significant result, however. It made the Civil War a fight for both the preservation of the Union and freedom for black Americans.

THE ELECTIONS OF 1863 AND 1864

In the state and local elections of 1863 the Republicans, who now called their party the Union party, made up for many of the losses they had suffered in 1862. They defeated outspoken Copperhead Democrats in races for governor of Pennsylvania and Ohio, and made substantial gains in California, New York, and the New England states. The Republicans couldn't afford to relax, however. In 1864 the country was scheduled to hold a presidential election. Holding national elections in the midst of a civil war was a risky business. Most northerners believed, however, that the failure to hold regularly scheduled elections would amount to an admission of defeat— something they were not prepared to do.

Lincoln's reelection in 1864 was far from certain. Some Radical Republicans, believing that Lincoln was moving too slowly in fighting the war, challenged his nomination. Nevertheless, the Union party's national convention nominated Lincoln for reelection by an overwhelming majority. The party also tried to widen its base of support by nominating a southern former Democrat, Andrew Johnson, for vice president.

The Democrats, meanwhile, nominated a Peace Democrat, former Union general George B. McClellan, for president. Although they declared their loyalty to the Union, the Democrats also called for the earliest possible end to the war. This suggested that if elected, McClellan would be willing to recognize the Confederacy's independence.

Although both parties campaigned vigorously, it seems likely that the 1864 election was actually decided on the battlefields, where Union armies drove deep into Confederate territory. In any event, the Union party won a decisive victory. Lincoln was reelected with 212 electoral votes, while McClellan received only 21. The Union party also won big victories in the congressional and state elections.

In the aftermath of their lopsided victory, few Republicans gave much thought to the wisdom of their choice for vice president. After all, Lincoln, who was in good health, could be expected to live many more years. Yet less than two months after Lincoln took office for a second term, he was dead from an assassin's bullet, and his vice president, Andrew Johnson, became president.

THE REPUBLICANS
AND DEMOCRATS AFTER
THE CIVIL WAR

Events in April 1865 struck the country with the force of an avalanche. General Robert E. Lee, who commanded the main Confederate army, surrendered to Union General Ulysses S. Grant. The Confederate government collapsed, and its leaders scattered. A pro-Confederate actor, John Wilkes Booth, shot President Lincoln to death. And Andrew Johnson, the former Democrat from Tennessee, faced the daunting task of putting the Union back together.

Johnson believed that the southern states should be restored to their former place in the Union as quickly as possible. His first step in restoring civil governments in those states was the appointment of temporary governors with the authority to organize conventions to write new state constitutions. Johnson imposed only two conditions: The new state officials must take an oath of future loyalty to the Union, and the states must outlaw slavery. In an effort to restore sectional harmony he also pardoned many former high-level Confederate military and civilian officials. To the dismay of many northerners, the voters in the southern states elected a number of these men to the new state governments and to Congress.

Although most Republicans agreed with the president's goal of restoring civil governments in the South, they drew the line at allowing the Confederate leaders to regain their former political power in the national government. They therefore refused to seat the new southern congressmen. The president and Congress were soon engaged in a fierce power struggle over the control of the restoration of the southern states to full participation in the national government—a process known as Reconstruction. Johnson repeatedly vetoed Congress's Reconstruction bills, and Congress promptly overrode his vetoes. Goaded by the president's refusal to cooperate in enforcing these laws, Congress adopted more severe measures to deal with the former Confederate states. In 1867, Congress imposed military rule in the South, and insisted that the southern states ratify the Fourteenth Amendment and give voting rights to blacks before the states could be represented in Congress.

Congress passed the Fourteenth Amendment in 1866 primarily to protect the rights of southern blacks and to prevent high-level Confederate officials from dominating the national government. President Johnson opposed the amendment because he did not believe that Congress had the authority to pass a constitutional amendment while the southern states were deprived of representation in Congress. During the summer of 1866 he campaigned for the election of candidates who opposed the ratification of the amendment. He also encouraged the formation of a new political party, the National Union party, to support his views on Reconstruction. The president's efforts were unsuccessful. The new party never really developed, and the Republicans retained their large majority in Congress.

THE IMPEACHMENT OF ANDREW JOHNSON

The battle between Andrew Johnson and Congress culminated in February 1868, when the Republicans in the House of Representatives tried to remove the president from office by a process called impeachment. The House may impeach a president (charge him with misconduct in office) by a majority vote of its members. The Senate then conducts a trial, after which it can remove the president from office by a two-thirds vote of its members.

The main charges against Andrew Johnson involved his violation of the Tenure of Office Act. Congress had passed this law in 1867 to stop the president from removing from office federal officials who refused to cooperate with him in obstructing the enforcement of the Reconstruction laws. The Tenure of Office Act forbade the president from removing from office any officials whose appointment required confirmation by the Senate without its consent. In February 1868 the president removed Secretary of War Edwin M. Stanton from office because Stanton was persistently undermining the president's Reconstruction policies. It was not clear whether the Tenure of Office Act applied to Cabinet officials. Some people believed that its application to Cabinet officials was a violation of the president's constitutional right to choose his own advisers. Others argued that regardless of his personal beliefs about the Tenure of Office Act, the president had no right to refuse to obey a law passed by Congress. (This issue was finally settled in 1926, when the Supreme Court held that the Senate's right to confirm the appointment of certain federal officials did not carry with it the right to consent to their removal.)

Regardless of the merits of the charges, the removal of an American president from office, which threatens the entire American system of government, can result in a political upheaval. In 1868, with the Civil War still fresh in people's minds, the Senate decided not to take this risk. After the conclusion of Johnson's trial, thirty-five senators voted to convict him, but nineteen, including seven Republicans, voted to acquit him of the charges the House had made. The Senate's vote was one less than the two-thirds majority needed to remove the president from office.

THE END OF RECONSTRUCTION AND THE DEMOCRATIC "REDEEMERS"

Shortly after the Senate had failed to remove President Johnson from office, Congress admitted seven southern states to full participation in the national government following their ratification of the Fourteenth Amendment. The three remaining southern states were admitted in 1870. (Tennessee had been admitted in 1866.) However, federal military forces remained in some parts of the South until 1877 to protect blacks against violence by whites.

During the Reconstruction period the Republicans dominated the southern governments. These governments removed the voting rights of many white southerners who had supported the Confeder-

With the end of Reconstruction in the South came a "changing of the guard." No longer would Union troops be present to uphold the voting rights of blacks and the agenda of the northern Republicans. This 1879 cartoon by Thomas Nast shows a Confederate soldier, representing the South, ready to take over the responsibility of "keeping the peace" at the polls, implying that the term meant different things to the different governments.

acy. The presence of Union troops, the loyalty of black voters to the Republican party, and the support of white southerners who had opposed secession helped the Republicans to retain their political power. But after the readmission of the Confederate states and the withdrawal of Union troops, it proved impossible to keep white southerners who opposed the Reconstruction governments from eventually driving the Republicans from office.

In their campaign to "redeem" the South from Republican rule, conservative white southerners claimed that the Republican governments were dominated by greedy northerners (called carpetbaggers), corrupt white southerners (called scalawags), and unqualified blacks, while many whites were deprived of their political rights. The Redeemers also used both economic pressure and intimidation to force blacks to refrain from voting or to vote for the Democratic party's candidates. One by one the southern states fell into line. Tennessee and Virginia went Democratic in 1869. Other southern states quickly followed, and Redemption was completed in 1877 when Florida, Louisiana, and South Carolina fell under Democratic control. The completion of the Democratic Redemption began a period of one-party rule in the South that lasted until the middle of the twentieth century.

REPUBLICANS AND DEMOCRATS IN THE NORTH

The Democrats in the North were badly hurt by the Civil War. For almost twenty years after the war ended, the Republicans won presidential elections by reminding the voters that their sacrifices on the battlefields had saved the Union—a tactic that was called "waving the bloody shirt." The Republicans also controlled Congress until 1874, when the Democrats gained a majority in the House of Representatives. Afterward, control of Congress changed hands several times during the rest of the nineteenth century. In general, however, the Democrats controlled the House, while the Republicans controlled the Senate.

During this period the symbols used to depict the two major political parties—the donkey for the Democrats and the elephant for the Republicans— became popular. Thomas Nast, whose political cartoons appeared in *Harper's Weekly*, helped to popularize these symbols. Both public interest in politics and party loyalties were strong, and party membership often extended from one generation to the next. Voting was a public event in which the voters placed cards, called tickets, containing the names of a party's candidates in the ballot box. The parties often

In an early use of the symbol, this Thomas Nast
cartoon depicts an injured Republican elephant
after the party's hard-fought victory in the
election of 1876, in which Rutherford B. Hayes
was elected president.

printed their tickets in different colors, so that people could easily tell which party's ticket they used. Voter turnout usually was high, averaging about three-quarters of the eligible voters. Party officials made sure of that by rounding up party members and seeing that they got to the polling places. Often the party members marched to the polls in military fashion, singing party songs or shouting party slogans. The party leaders also made sure that every member received the party's ticket, and watched to see who dropped it into the ballot box. The use of different colored tickets made it easy for party leaders to see who voted "right."

POLITICAL CORRUPTION

Both major political parties were guilty of political corruption, which was rampant throughout the country at all levels of government during the last half of the nineteenth century. Political power was often in the hands of men who had not been elected to public office. Party bosses—men who led political organizations based on the distribution of political patronage and the granting of political favors—controlled many city governments. Business interests often controlled the state legislatures and had a significant influence over Congress, especially the Senate, whose members were chosen by the state legislatures. Bribery, threats, and the use of political patronage enabled a few individuals to maintain political and economic power at the expense of the general public. The Democrats' insistence on a limited role for the federal government and the Republicans' desire to aid American businesses made both parties close their eyes to the corruption.

THE LIBERAL REPUBLICANS

Political corruption was especially widespread during the presidency of Ulysses S. Grant. The Republicans had nominated the popular Civil War general for the election of 1868. Although his popular-vote majority was small, Grant easily defeated his Democratic opponent, Horace Seymour (a former governor of New York), in the electoral-vote count. The rampant corruption during Grant's first term of office caused some Republicans to rebel against the president. After failing to stop Grant's nomination for reelection in 1872, the group formed a new political party, the Liberal Republican party. Both the Liberal Republicans and the Democrats nominated Horace Greeley, an eccentric newspaper editor, for president. Despite mounting evidence of corruption during his first term as president, Grant won an over-

Ulysses S. Grant may have been a popular
Civil War hero, but his two terms as president
were plagued by corruption. The caption of this
1880 cartoon from *Puck*, a publication of the
time, read: "[We] want a strong man at the
head of government but not this kind."

whelming victory over Greeley, who died shortly after the election. After the election of 1872, the Liberal Republican party disbanded, but its members continued to work for political reforms.

THE ELECTION OF 1876

The issue of political corruption came to a head during the presidential election of 1876. The Republican candidate was Ohio Governor Rutherford B. Hayes. The Democratic candidate was Samuel J. Tilden of New York. Tilden had won political fame for his work in overthrowing one of the country's earliest and most corrupt political bosses, New York City's William Marcy Tweed. Tilden won a majority of the popular votes. However, claims of voting fraud by both Republicans and Democrats left the electoral votes of three southern states—Florida, Louisiana, and South Carolina—in doubt. (Although the Democratic Redeemers were on the verge of taking control of the governments of these states, they remained in Republican hands at the time of the election of 1876.) Congress, hoping to end widespread fears of a renewal of the Civil War, appointed a special fifteen-member electoral commission composed of seven Democrats and eight Republicans to resolve the dispute. The commission eventually awarded all the electoral votes in these states to Hayes, making him president by a majority of only one electoral vote.

THE ELECTION OF 1884

The issue of political corruption surfaced again in the election of 1884, when many former Liberal Republicans helped to elect a Democratic president, Grover Cleveland, over the Republican candidate, James G. Blaine. These Republican deserters, often called Mugwumps, were unhappy over Blaine's past record of political corruption. Cleveland failed to win reelection in 1888, however. Although he won a majority of the popular votes, his Republican opponent, Benjamin Harrison, won a majority of the electoral votes due to narrow victories in several heavily populated northern states. The Republicans also gained control of Congress.

During President Harrison's first two years in office the Republican Congress spent so lavishly in an attempt to gain political support that many people scornfully called it the Billion-Dollar Congress. A widespread public outcry against the free-spending Republicans allowed the Democrats to regain control of the House in 1890. In 1892, Grover Cleveland won a second term as president, and the Democrats took control of both houses of Congress.

TWO LATE NINETEENTH-CENTURY REFORMS

Public concern over political corruption after the Civil War led to two political reforms that affected the future course of American politics. One was civil-service reform. The other was the adoption of the secret ballot.

In 1883, after a deranged man who had failed to win a political appointment assassinated Republican President James A. Garfield, Congress passed the Civil Service Act. Liberal Republicans, who wanted to end the corruption associated with political patronage, had urged the enactment of civil-service reform for some time. Some Democrats joined them in this effort in the hope of lessening the Republican control over political patronage. After the assassination of Garfield, his Republican successor, Chester A. Arthur, endorsed civil-service reform. The Civil Service Act, which was first introduced in 1880 by a Democratic senator, George Hunt Pendleton of Ohio, required that some federal jobs be given based on merit instead of political party membership. The law also forbade political parties from demanding contributions from federal employees to finance election campaigns—a practice that was widespread at that time. Although they helped to make the federal workforce less dependent on political party affiliation and more efficient, these restrictions reduced the ability of the political parties to give political rewards to loyal party members and to seek contributions from them. As a result, the parties had to raise money from other sources.

During the last two decades of the nineteenth century some state and local governments began using the secret ballot to reduce political corruption. By 1896 the secret ballot was used in about 90 percent of the states. Instead of allowing the political parties to use their own ballots, the states printed and distributed ballots containing the names of all candidates for public office. Voters could then mark the ballots to indicate their choices. Secret balloting made it easier for voters to engage in so-called ticket splitting, or voting for the candidates of different political parties in one election. By reducing the ability of party officials to observe how people voted, the secret ballot also reduced the parties' control over elections, although it did not completely stop voting fraud.

The enactment of civil-service reform and the adoption of secret balloting did not end the political reform movement, however. During the late nineteenth and early twentieth centuries forces were at work that would lead to major changes in American politics.

THE AGE OF REFORM:
THE POPULIST AND
PROGRESSIVE PARTIES

The rapid industrialization of the North after the Civil War resulted in a widening gulf between the rich and poor. Industrial workers in the cities, many of whom were recent immigrants, crowded into unsanitary and unsafe housing. They often worked long hours for low wages under hazardous conditions, while the industrial leaders accumulated enormous wealth.

Small farmers in the South and West were not much better off. These farmers, who often depended on credit extended by local merchants to survive from one planting season to the next, were generally

93

burdened with debts that grew every year despite their best efforts to cut expenses. Moreover, small farmers who shipped their crops to nearby cities for marketing were often the victims of discriminatory practices by the railroads.

The search for ways to improve these conditions eventually led to the formation of new political parties. Two of the most influential of these parties were the People's (or Populist) party and the Progressive (or Bull Moose) party.

THE FARMERS' ALLIANCE

The People's party grew out of an organization of Texas farmers called the Farmers' Alliance. The Alliance, which was formed in 1878 to deal with the problems of small farmers, quickly spread into other southern states, the Midwest, and the western plains. At first the Alliance members worked to obtain reforms through their own political parties—the Democrats in the South and the Republicans in the Midwest and West. They proposed a number of political and economic reforms and pushed for the election of candidates who supported their proposals.

In 1890, Alliance candidates defeated the regular Democratic party candidates in several southern states and seriously threatened Democratic control in others. Alliance candidates also won state elections as well as a number of congressional elections in the western plains states.

THE PEOPLE'S PARTY AND THE OMAHA PLATFORM

Encouraged by these successes, Alliance leaders met at St. Louis, Missouri, in February 1892 to form the People's party. In July delegates met at Omaha, Nebraska, for the party's first national convention. The party's platform contained a ringing condemnation of both the Republicans and Democrats. The platform accused both parties of struggling for "power and plunder, while grievous wrongs have been inflicted upon the suffering people." The Populists then declared: "We believe that the powers of government—in other words, of the people—should be expanded . . . as rapidly and as far as the good sense of an intelligent people and the teachings of experience shall justify, to the end that oppression, injustice, and poverty shall eventually cease in the land."[5]

The Populists then demanded a number of reforms, including the unlimited coinage of silver, the lowering of tariffs, a tax on individual incomes, government ownership of the railroads, and the establishment of the secret ballot (already in use in some states). The platform also called for constitutional amendments to limit the president and vice president to one term in office, and to elect U.S. senators by popular vote instead of by the state legislatures.

Many of the statements in the Omaha Platform seemed truly radical to nineteenth-century Americans. Both the Republicans and the Democrats denounced the Populists as a pack of dangerous lunatics. The People's party had high hopes for the future, however. In the election of 1892 its presidential candidate, James B. Weaver, received more than a million popular votes and twenty-two electoral votes—a promising showing for a party that had been born only a few months earlier.

The Populists continued to gain ground in the South in the elections of 1894. However, the party's strength was still confined to a few rural areas. Despite their efforts to form an alliance with working-class Americans, the Populists failed to gain the support of the factory workers in the industrial areas of the Northeast. There were several reasons for this failure. One was that the industrial workers had little in common with the small farmers. Another was the refusal of the emerging labor unions, such as the American Federation of Labor, to engage in political activity. (It would be more than forty years before labor unions became active in American politics.) Finally, many immigrant factory workers, who had become Socialists in Europe, joined the new Socialist groups in the United States. (The Socialists were never very influential in American politics, however. Their advocacy of public ownership of transportation, communications, and natural resources conflicted with the belief of most Americans in free enterprise and private property.)

THE FREE-SILVER ISSUE

Meanwhile, the idea of the unlimited coinage of silver was growing in popularity. The free-silver issue had surfaced in 1873, when the government stopped issuing silver dollars. Members of Congress from silver mining states later pushed through laws requiring the government to buy silver. The latest of these laws, the Sherman Silver Purchase Act of 1890, required the government to buy 4.5 million ounces (128 million grams) of silver each month, paid for by treasury notes called silver certificates, which could be exchanged for coins. Many people who preferred gold coins to paper money turned in their silver certificates, thus reducing the amount of money in circulation instead of increasing it as Congress intended.

In 1893 a financial panic resulted in a massive withdrawal of gold from the treasury. President Grover Cleveland, who believed (as did most Americans at that time) that economic stability depended on a currency backed by sufficient gold reserves, persuaded a reluctant Congress to repeal the Sherman Silver Purchase Act. Cleveland hoped that this would stop the outflow of gold from the treasury and restore the health of the economy. Conditions worsened, however. A severe depression gripped the country, causing widespread unemployment and labor unrest, some of which resulted in violence. The economic hardships also spurred renewed demands for the unlimited coinage of silver.

The free-silver issue split the Populists. Many Populists believed that the amount of silver coins in circulation was only part of the problem. They thought that the real problem was the inadequate money supply (whether in gold, silver, or some other medium) that kept small farmers in debt and ensured the power of the eastern bankers and industrial leaders to shape American policies. However, a growing number of politically experienced Populists believed that the free-silver issue would help them to win the next national election.

THE ELECTION OF 1896 AND THE DEATH OF THE PEOPLE'S PARTY

The free-silver issue also split both the Democrats and Republicans. In 1896 the Democrats nominated a free-silver advocate, William Jennings Bryan of Nebraska, for president. A group of conservative

The Free-Silver issue split the Democratic party
in the 1896 presidential election. This cartoon
suggests that western Free-Silver advocates had
captured the party and were controlling it.
In pursuit were the sound money Democrats.

Democrats who opposed the free coinage of silver then organized the National Democratic party, which nominated John M. Palmer of Illinois for president. The Republicans nominated Ohio Governor William McKinley on a platform that endorsed "sound money"—money backed by sufficient gold reserves—and opposed a return to the issuance of silver coins. A Republican faction favoring free silver then formed the National Silver party, which nominated Bryan.

Shortly after the Democratic convention, the Populists also nominated Bryan over the heated objections of those who wanted the party to name its own candidate. These Populists warned that if the Populists agreed to a joint Populist-Democrat nominee, the Democrats would eventually swallow the People's party, just as major political parties had absorbed many third parties in the past. This warning proved to be prophetic. As it turned out, the Populist party was eventually absorbed into the Democratic party.

The Populists influenced the future course of the Democratic party, however. This influence could be seen in the Democratic platform of 1896. Although starting with a restatement of the Democrats' traditional belief in a federal government that exercised only those powers specifically granted under the Constitution, the platform demanded the passage of laws to protect the rights of American labor, which "creates the wealth of the country," and the imposition of restrictions on the railroads to "protect the people from robbery and oppression."[6]

The Democrat-Populist ticket suffered a major defeat in the election of 1896. The Republican candidate, McKinley, easily defeated all of his opponents. Moreover, the Republicans, who had recaptured Congress from the Democrats in 1894, increased their majority in that body. The Republican victory in 1896 marked a political realignment, which resulted in Republican dominance of national politics that continued almost without interruption until 1932.

The People's party continued to have a marginal existence for a few years after the election of 1896. In 1908 the remnants of the party nominated its last presidential candidate, Thomas E. Watson of Georgia. In 1912 the party formally disbanded. Meanwhile, another group of reformers, called Progressives, was at work.

THE PROGRESSIVES

The term "Progressives" is generally used to refer to the people who worked for reforms during the first two decades of the twentieth century. The Progressives did not start out as a political party. Many of them were Republicans in the tradition of the Liberal Republicans and Mugwumps of the late nineteenth century. There were also Democrats from the Bryan wing of the Democratic party. The Progressives included many affluent, well-educated professionals who lived in the nation's large urban areas. As such, they had a wider base of support than the Populists, whose strength lay mainly in sparsely populated rural regions. The Progressives shared the prevailing belief among educated Americans that the government, aided by the new professional class, should use its powers to eliminate social ills. Despite their desire for a greater role for the government in American society, they generally disliked political parties, which they regarded as sources of political corruption, and worked to reduce their power.

The Progressives were instrumental in persuading some state legislatures to hold primary elections in which voters could choose their party's candidates for public office instead of allowing the party leaders to make the selections. They also got many states to establish procedures by which voters could initiate state legislation (the initiative) and vote on laws the state legislatures had already passed (the referendum). In addition, they obtained reforms designed to make city governments more efficient and less subject to the will of party bosses. One such reform was the establishment of nonpartisan commissions staffed by professional experts to regulate public transportation, public utilities, and similar enterprises. The Progressives didn't have much success in national politics, however, until Theodore Roosevelt became president.

THEODORE ROOSEVELT AND THE PROGRESSIVE PARTY

Theodore Roosevelt, a hero of the Spanish-American War of 1898, was the Republican nominee for vice president in 1900, when William McKinley successfully sought a second term as president. (McKinley's first vice president, Garret A. Hobart, had died in 1899.) After McKinley's assassination in September 1901, Roosevelt became president. Young Teddy Roosevelt, who was only forty-two years old when he became president, was enormously popular. He was elected to his own term as president in 1904 by a large electoral- and popular-vote majority.

Although Roosevelt initially held fairly conservative views on political issues, he had adopted many of the Progressive beliefs by the time he became president. During his presidency Roosevelt persuaded Congress to pass laws to regulate railroad charges, ensure the purity of commercially packaged food and medicines, and conserve America's natural resources. At the same time the federal government successfully

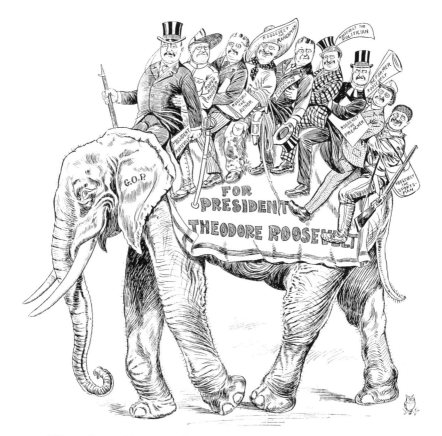

**Theodore Roosevelt was a very popular political
figure who easily won the election of 1904.
As this cartoon suggests, Roosevelt wore many
hats, so to speak, and cast himself as everyman
through the widely varied causes he took on.**

sued several major business combinations, called
trusts, for unlawfully blocking competition.

In 1908, Roosevelt, who declined to seek reelection, backed his secretary of war, William Howard
Taft, for the Republican presidential nomination. In

the election of 1908, Taft handily defeated William Jennings Bryan, who was making his third and last run for the presidency.

During Taft's administration Congress passed two of the Populists' recommended reforms—constitutional amendments that provided for income taxes and the direct election of U.S. senators. These amendments became part of the Constitution in 1913. Taft's administration was largely conservative in tone, however. Taft, who had a narrow view of presidential powers, did little to stop conservative members of Congress from passing laws that conflicted with the Republicans' platform of 1908. Taft's conservative policies caused a major rift in the Republican party, pitting old-line conservatives against the Progressives.

Taft's actions as president caused Roosevelt to challenge him for the 1912 Republican presidential nomination. Although Roosevelt defeated Taft in a few states that held primary elections, Taft won in the rest of the states, where party leaders, who were largely old-line conservatives, controlled the selection of delegates to the party's national convention. Roosevelt's supporters challenged the selection of about 250 delegates who had agreed to vote for Taft. The Republican National Committee awarded most of the contested seats to Taft supporters, giving Taft enough votes to ensure his nomination. Roosevelt's backers, declaring that Taft had stolen the nomination, then held their own convention in which they formed the National Progressive party and nominated Roosevelt for president. The new party was promptly nicknamed the Bull Moose party because of a statement by Roosevelt that he felt as fit as a bull moose.

Although the Progressive party included some experienced politicians, most Republicans, including some who had backed Roosevelt for the Republican nomination, decided to support the Republican candidates rather than risk their own political careers by joining a new party. As a result, the Progressive party leadership was divided between professional politicians and reformers who did not hold public office, such as college professors, social workers, and crusaders for various causes.

THE ELECTION OF 1912

The Democratic presidential nominee in 1912 was New Jersey Governor Woodrow Wilson, a former president of Princeton University. During the 1912 election campaign Wilson reversed his earlier conservative stands on several political issues and endorsed Progressive reforms such as attempts to rein in the large corporations. Wilson's endorsement of Progressive reforms, together with the fear of many Republicans that the Progressive party was really a means for Roosevelt to regain his own personal power, drew enough Republican votes to enable Wilson to win an electoral-vote landslide. Roosevelt came in second, and Taft a poor third.

Wilson, like Roosevelt, was a strong president. Shortly after taking office, he persuaded Congress to enact drastic reductions in tariff rates. He also got Congress to enact a stronger law to curb the power of the large trusts to engage in unfair business practices. Perhaps his most significant accomplishment was a major reform of the nation's banking system. The Federal Reserve Act, which Wilson signed into law in December 1913, created twelve regional Federal Reserve Banks under the direction of a Federal Reserve Board with the authority to regulate the amount of money in circulation. The law wasn't effective in preventing major economic crises, such as the Great Depression of the 1930s, but it did help in preventing the frequent financial panics that had disrupted the American economy in the past.

THE 1916 ELECTION AND THE DEATH OF THE PROGRESSIVE PARTY

In 1916 the Progressive party convention again nominated Theodore Roosevelt for president, but this time he refused to accept the nomination. Instead, he endorsed the Republican candidate, Supreme Court Justice Charles Evans Hughes, a former governor of New York. On Roosevelt's recommendation the national committee of the Progressive party also nominated Hughes. After Wilson defeated Hughes in a close election, the Progressive party, already torn between the professional politicians and the social reformers, collapsed. Most of its members followed Roosevelt back into the Republican party, while others became Democrats.

The Progressive reform impulse had largely played itself out by the mid-1920s. However, the efforts of the Progressives inspired later reformers to push for even greater changes during the 1930s. By that time both major parties had reversed their positions regarding the role of the federal government in American politics.

THE EMERGENCE OF
THE MODERN DEMOCRATIC
AND REPUBLICAN PARTIES

By the early part of the twentieth century both the Republicans and the Democrats generally agreed on the need for government regulation of business to curb the worst abuses by the huge trusts. Such regulations increased substantially after America's entry into World War I in 1917. As the nation mobilized for an all-out war effort, federal agencies directed the allocation of manpower, food, fuel, and other supplies, operated railroads and communication facilities, and supervised working conditions in most industries. President Woodrow Wilson justified this reversal of the traditional Democratic belief in limited government as a temporary wartime necessity.

The end of the war in November 1918 and the return of the Republicans to power in 1920 curtailed the federal government's massive intervention into the American economy. During the 1920s the Republicans adopted a policy of taxing and spending as little as possible, leaving the states and private businesses largely free from federal supervision. Encouraged by the booming economy, the voters elected Republican presidents in 1920, 1924, and 1928.

Moreover, the Republicans, who had taken control of Congress in 1918 after six years of Democratic control, kept a majority of congressional seats throughout most of the 1920s. However, by the end of the decade a Republican president, Herbert Hoover, had to deal with a severe economic depression that began after a stock market crash in October 1929.

In 1932, as the country struggled to cope with the deepening depression, Hoover's Democratic challenger, New York Governor Franklin D. Roosevelt (a distant cousin of Theodore Roosevelt) won an overwhelming popular and electoral-vote victory. The Democrats also won large majorities in both houses of Congress, ushering in another political realignment that gave the Democrats control of the presidency for the next twenty years and control of Congress, with minor interruptions, for more than fifty years.

THE NEW DEAL

After the Democratic national convention nominated him for president, Roosevelt established a new precedent by accepting the nomination in a speech before the convention delegates. During his speech Roosevelt promised to bring a "new deal" to the American people. The phrase caught on, and Roosevelt's administration became known as the New Deal.

After taking office, Roosevelt proposed a sweeping array of government programs to revive the ailing economy and to provide both temporary and long-term financial relief to individuals who were hurt by unemployment, old age, or the loss of the family breadwinner. Many of these proposals involved the creation of new federal agencies staffed by an army of employees, thus greatly expanding the role of the federal government.

Congress enacted most of the New Deal programs even though the idea of spending federal tax money to help individual Americans was a radical departure from the traditional belief that such help was a matter for the states to handle. Eventually the Supreme Court upheld many of these laws on the grounds that they fell within the powers of Congress to regulate interstate commerce and to tax and spend for the general welfare.

Some of the many federal agencies created
under Franklin D. Roosevelt's New Deal are
pictured here as raucous children dancing
around the gleeful president. Among them are
the Works Progress Administration (WPA), the
Public Works Administration (PWA), and the
Agricultural Adjustment Administration (AAA).

WORLD WAR II AND THE THIRD TERM CONTROVERSY

The American entry into World War II in December 1941 resulted in control by the federal government over virtually every aspect of the economy, just as it had during World War I in Woodrow Wilson's administration. The war, which started in 1939, also led to a break with a political tradition dating from George Washington's presidency—that of a president not seeking a third term.

In 1940, as the country drifted toward war, the Democrats nominated Roosevelt for a third term. His decision to accept the nomination was controversial. Most Republicans and some Democrats opposed it both because it was a break with a time-honored tradition and because they feared that Roosevelt would try to establish himself as a dictator. The popular president won both a third and a fourth term, however, remaining in office until his death in April 1945. Meanwhile, the Republicans, who didn't want to seem disloyal during the war, were reduced to echoing the wartime proposals of the Democrats.

The New Deal era of the 1930s completed a reversal of the positions of the two parties on the role of the federal government—a reversal that began in 1896, when the Democratic platform took the first tentative steps toward an endorsement of government action to support the interests of ordinary Americans. During the 1930s the Democrats, once the party of limited government, adopted an expansive view of the powers of the federal government to deal with virtually every social, economic, and political problem the nation might encounter. The Republicans, on the other hand, who had once used federal money to finance economic development and to help the former slaves to adjust to their new freedom, now endorsed the idea of a federal government that could exercise only those powers specifically assigned to it by the Constitution.

Although by the 1930s the Democrats and Republicans had reversed their stands on the role of the federal government, their views on this question weren't hard and fast. Conservative southern Democrats, who clung to the idea of states' rights, often joined the Republicans in opposing Democratic measures. Also, in later years both parties accepted the idea of federal responsibility for social welfare, although they differed on how and to what extent this responsibility should be exercised.

CRACKS IN THE SOLID SOUTH

The Democratic coalition that brought Franklin D. Roosevelt to power in 1932 included city residents (many of whom were descended from nineteenth-century immigrants), labor union members, and white southerners who wanted to maintain one-party rule in the South. In 1936 the coalition broadened to include northern blacks, most of whom had remained loyal to the Republican party long after the end of Reconstruction. (At that time few southern blacks could vote.) However, in later years increasing numbers of white southern conservatives joined the Republican party. This trend wasn't surprising, considering the shift by Republicans to positions that favored states' rights and a limited federal government.

In 1928 the first cracks appeared in the Democratic dominance of the "Solid South" that had lasted since the end of the Reconstruction period. In 1928 many Americans in urban areas wanted to repeal the Eighteenth Amendment, which outlawed the manufacture and sale of alcoholic beverages. These city residents, who were largely descended from nineteenth-century Irish and German immigrants, voted heavily Democratic in the 1928 elections. However, the Democratic party's support for the repeal of Prohibition, combined with its nomination of a Roman Catholic, Albert E. Smith, for president, caused many conservative southerners to desert the party. Their desertion helped the Republicans to win the electoral votes of five former Confederate states—Florida, North Carolina, Tennessee, Texas, and Virginia. In 1932 the southern Democrats resumed their former loyalty to their party, however.

Although the Solid South remained Democratic throughout Franklin D. Roosevelt's presidency, new cracks emerged in 1948, when northern liberals forced the acceptance of a Democratic plank favoring the enactment of civil-rights laws to protect black Americans. Southern Democrats, angry over the civil-rights plank, formed the States' Rights party. Its presidential candidate, Strom Thurmond of South Carolina, won the electoral votes of four former Confederate states—Alabama, Louisiana, Mississippi, and South Carolina. However, these votes weren't enough to stop President Harry S. Truman, who had assumed that office on Roosevelt's death, from winning a term of office in his own right.

In 1952 the Solid South cracked again when the Republican presidential candidate, Dwight D. Eisenhower, who had commanded the Allied military forces during World War II, captured the electoral votes of Florida, Tennessee, Texas, and Virginia. The Republican trend in the South continued in later years. In 1968 the Democratic presidential candidate, Hubert H. Humphrey, carried only one former Confederate state, Texas. Similarly, in 1980, President Jimmy Carter, who lost to his Republican challenger, Ronald Reagan, carried only one southern state, his home state of Georgia, and in 1984, Reagan swept the South in a landslide victory over the Democratic candidate, Walter Mondale.

Today many southern states have elected Republican governors, state legislators, and members of Congress. The Democrats are still competitive in the South, however. The Voting Rights Act of 1965, which restored the voting rights of black southerners, has helped southern black Democrats, who are among the party's most loyal supporters, to win offices in state and local governments as well as Congress.

CHANGES IN ELECTION CAMPAIGNS

Both the Republicans and the Democrats have made many changes in their conduct of election campaigns since the turn of the century. Advances in transportation and communication are responsible for many of the changes. Presidential candidates, who now campaign openly instead of following the old practice of not actively seeking the office, travel long distances in an effort to win votes. The old practice of staging rallies, parades, and picnics to stir up enthusiasm for a party's candidates gradually gave way to professionally directed campaigns featuring paid speakers and campaign literature explaining that party's position on current issues. This practice was later replaced by campaigns that use advertising techniques to "sell" a candidate through paid advertisements and speeches on radio and television.

THE EFFECT OF TELEVISION ON ELECTION CAMPAIGNS

The advent of commercial television after World War II brought major changes in the conduct of election campaigns. The election of 1948 brought the first televised coverage of the Republican and Democratic national conventions, which gave millions of viewers a renewed taste of the political spectacle that had entertained voters during the nineteenth century. The first few televised conventions contained suspense as well as spectacle. The winner of the nomination was often in doubt until after one or more rounds of voting took place. However, in later years a substantial increase in presidential primary elections made the nominations virtually certain long before the party conventions met. The public gradually lost interest in the conventions, and in 1996 the television networks responded to the decline in viewers by drastic cutbacks in their convention coverage.

In 1960 the first televised debates between presidential candidates took place. During these debates the youthful, handsome Democratic candidate, Massachusetts Senator John F. Kennedy, offered viewers a sharp contrast with the haggard, unshaven appearance of the Republican candidate, Vice President Richard M. Nixon, who had been ill earlier in the year. It is not clear how much Kennedy's personal appearance influenced the voters. However, he won a very close election that hinged on the electoral votes of Illinois and Texas.

Television soon became a major part of presidential election campaigns. Televised debates, news items on the evening newscasts, televised speeches, and paid television advertisements dominated those campaigns.

CHANGES IN CAMPAIGN FINANCING

All the changes in election campaigns combined to increase their costs. The political parties, which had once relied on contributions from party members, especially those who benefited from political patronage, increasingly sought contributions from wealthy supporters and business interests that stood to benefit from a party's election victory. Later, mass mailings and telephone calls were used to solicit contributions from party members and the general public.

The corruption associated with corporate donations to political parties eventually forced the adoption of reforms such as the direct election of U.S. senators. Both Congress and the state legislatures have passed laws to regulate campaign financing. These laws are easy to evade, however.

In 1974, Republican violations of campaign financing laws as well as evidence of other misdeeds led to the resignation of President Nixon to avoid impeachment, making him the first American president to resign from office. The so-called Watergate scandal resulted in further restrictions on campaign financing, but did not end the power of money to influence (and perhaps to dominate) American elections.

The election of 1968 ushered in another change in American politics—the prevalence of divided government. During most of the period from 1968 to 1992 the country had a Republican president and a Democratic Congress. (This situation was reversed in 1994, when the Republicans took control of Congress, while a Democrat, Bill Clinton, was president.) The frequent deadlocks resulting from divided government led many Americans to question whether either major party was capable of effective government. The widespread dissatisfaction seemed to indicate that the country was ripe for another political realignment, perhaps involving the formation of a new political party to replace one or both major parties.

CHAPTER 10

THIRD PARTIES AND THE AMERICAN TWO-PARTY SYSTEM

In 1992 a Texas billionaire, H. Ross Perot, decided to run for president as the head of a third party. Using his own money, Perot conducted a series of television programs in which he argued for drastic political reforms. Using charts and graphs to illustrate his points, he showed how the tendency of both major parties to spend more money than the government takes in each year can eventually result in its inability to pay its bills. Perot's message persuaded almost one-fifth of American voters to vote for his Reform party in 1992. Despite this impressive showing, Perot failed to win

The most successful third-party candidate of
modern times, Ross Perot was a prominent figure
in the presidential elections of 1992 and 1996.
This cartoon from 1995 depicts Perot as a
volcano that seems to erupt every four years, spew-
ing steam out of his ears and the top of his head.

even one electoral vote. Moreover, his share of the popular vote fell to 8 percent in the election of 1996.

Perot's Reform party was fairly typical of third parties in the United States. Many third parties have arisen in the past as Americans reacted to various problems. Most of these parties lasted through only one or two presidential elections and rarely won any electoral votes.

There are many reasons for the poor showing of third parties. Some relate to the weaknesses of the parties. For example, many third parties were formed to deal with a single issue or with policies that affect only a small part of the population. Without a broad base of support, these parties stood little chance of winning national elections. Another problem has been the difficulty of persuading prominent persons to run for office on a third-party ticket. Moreover, third parties have often been dominated by reformers with little or no experience in practical politics.

Third parties, also, have faced external obstacles in achieving their goals. One is the hostility of the major parties, which often regard third parties as threats to their own political power. In addition, the electoral-vote system, by enabling a candidate to win all of a state's electoral votes with the thinnest of majorities in that state, often prevents third-party candidates from effectively competing for the presidency.

Although the two major parties have generally succeeded in fending off third-party challengers, during the twentieth century many other competing forces have emerged to challenge their dominance of American government.

One of these forces is the existence of special-interest groups that try to influence elections and public policies. Interest groups have existed throughout most of our history. Such groups have included the abolitionists, the Prohibitionists, and the crusaders for voting rights for blacks and women. In recent years, however, interest groups have increased both in number and zeal. Today's interest groups include the National Organization for Women, the American Association of Retired Persons, the National Rifle Association, labor union political action committees, religious groups such as the Christian Coalition, and numerous organizations representing various business interests. Many of these groups rival the major political parties in size, fundraising ability, and influence on American politics.

Another major force that challenges the political parties is the mass communications news media, especially television. We have already examined the influence of televised debates and paid political advertising on elections. Television journalists have also become increasingly influential. Television newscasts and newsmagazines can influence the discussion of political issues by deciding both what news items to report and how to report them.

The advent of television and the increase in presidential primaries have also resulted in campaigns that focus on the candidate rather than the issues and the political parties. Although political parties can provide both financial and other help to individual candidates, an attractive individual with substantial financial backing can win the nomination of a major party without relying on the party for personal endorsement or financial support. In fact, given the widespread distaste of the American public for political parties, a candidate can often gain a significant advantage by running as an "outsider"— a person who is not tarred by the corruption associated with partisan politics. Sometimes candidates claim to be political outsiders because they have never held national office (and presumably have not been corrupted by Washington politics) even though they have had considerable experience in state and local politics.

A far more disturbing trend is a decline in the ability of the political parties to motivate the voters to cast their ballots on election day. During the past hundred years there has been a significant decline in voter turnout. In the election of 1896 almost 80 percent of the eligible voters cast their ballots. This dropped to 73 percent in 1900, and 65 percent in 1904. After that, the percentage held fairly steady until the early 1920s, when the turnout dropped to

NON-VOTERS OF THE PAST

NON-VOTERS OF THE PRESENT

VICTIMS OF RACISM

VICTIMS OF SEXISM

VICTIMS OF CYNICISM

Declining voter turnout indicates that political parties are neither attracting numbers to their ranks nor doing a sufficient job of motivating those already in their ranks to participate in elections. This cartoon reminds us that, political parties notwithstanding, for many in this country the right to vote was hard fought.

49 percent. The decline in the 1920s may have been due partly to the addition of women—many of whom initially did not go out and vote—to the group of eligible voters by the ratification of the Nineteenth Amendment in August 1920. However, voter turnout, although rising somewhat in later periods,

never again reached the levels of the nineteenth century. Moreover, the trend in recent years has been toward further declines in voter turnout. In 1980 only 52 percent of the eligible voters turned out, and only 51 percent of them voted for the winning candidate, Ronald Reagan. In 1996, President Clinton was reelected with 49 percent of the popular vote, while voter turnout dropped to an all-time low of less than 49 percent. Many explanations, including a widespread belief that Clinton's victory was assured long before the election, have been offered for the record low turnout in 1996. Whatever the reasons for the discouragingly low turnout, the fact remains that less than one-quarter of eligible voters elected Clinton to the most powerful office in the country, and perhaps in the world.

Despite its many weaknesses, however, the American two-party system has proved to be remarkably durable. The Republican party dates from the middle of the nineteenth century. The Democratic party is even older. The modern Democratic party was formed before the election of 1828. Many Democrats trace their origins to the Jeffersonian Republicans who opposed the Federalists toward the end of the eighteenth century. Major new parties such as the Republican party have emerged only rarely, and only two major parties—the Federalists and the Whigs—have gone out of existence in the past two centuries. This does not mean that political parties won't undergo major changes in the future. It could be argued that one (or even both) of today's major parties will someday cease to exist. If that happens, however, it seems certain that another new political party will emerge to take its place.

Americans have never had much respect for political parties. There is ample reason for such an attitude. Our history is filled with examples of political corruption. However, there are also examples of political leaders who displayed statesmanship, patriotism, and heroic devotion to principles regardless of personal cost. Moreover, whatever opinion we hold regarding political parties, one thing seems clear— we cannot do without them.

In the absence of a complete consensus on every major political issue—a virtual impossibility in a country as large and as diverse as the United States—some political combinations are inevitable. James Madison recognized this in January 1792, when he wrote in the Jeffersonian Republicans' newspaper, *National Gazette*, that in "every political society, parties are unavoidable."[7] Similarly, Thomas Jefferson, in a letter written in June 1798, stated that "in every free and deliberating society, there must, from the nature of man, be opposite parties. . . . Perhaps this party division is necessary to induce each to watch and relate to the people the proceedings of the other."[8] Martin Van Buren later argued that political parties not only are necessary but in the right hands can be a positive good for the country.

Whatever opinion we may hold about political parties, for better or worse, they are part and parcel of the American system of government—a system that for all its flaws has endured for more than two hundred years.

1. *Inaugural Addresses of the Presidents of the United States from George Washington 1789 to George Bush 1989, Bicentennial Edition* (Washington, DC: U.S. Government Printing Office, 1989), pp. 14–15.
2. Stanley Elkins and Eric McKitrick, *The Age of Federalism: The Early American Republic, 1788-1800* (New York: Oxford University Press, 1993), p. 754.
3. *Ibid.*
4. Noble Cunningham, *The Presidency of James Monroe* (Lawrence: University of Kansas Press, 1996), p. 189.
5. John D. Hicks, *The Populist Revolt: A History of the Farmers' Alliance and the People's Party* (1931; reprint, Lincoln: University of Nebraska Press, 1961), pp. 440–441.

6. Donald Bruce Johnson and Kirk H. Porter, comps., *National Party Platforms 1840–1972* (Urbana: University of Illinois Press, 1973), p. 99.
7. *The Age of Federalism*, p. 266.
8. Richard Hofstadter, *The Idea of a Party System: The Rise of Legitimate Opposition in the United States, 1780–1840* (Berkeley: University of California Press, 1969), p. 115.

aliens—persons who are not citizens of the country in which they live.

cabinet—a group of advisers chosen by the leader of a government to administer particular government departments.

canvassing—soliciting support in a particular area for a political party or its candidates.

caucus—a meeting of leaders or members of a political party to make plans, choose candidates, or decide how to vote on certain issues.

charter—a written grant by a state or national government giving certain rights or privileges to an organization.

electoral college—the group that elects the president and vice president of the United States.

electoral votes—the votes cast by members of the electoral college.

emancipation—the release from slavery or other restraints on an individual's personal liberty.

federal government—the national government of the United States.

federalism—a system of government in which power is divided between the states and the national government, with each having control over specific aspects of government.

impeachment—a formal charge of misconduct against a public official.

initiative—a process under which a state's voters may propose new laws without the legislature's action.

nativism—bias against persons who were born in foreign countries.

nullification—a declaration that a particular action is not binding or has no effect, such as a formal decision by a state that it is no longer obligated to obey a federal law.

override—to prevail over or set aside. Congress may override a president's veto of a bill by a two-thirds majority of both of its houses.

partisan—pertaining to a political party.

plank—a political party's written statement of its position regarding a specific issue. A group of planks makes up the party's platform.

platform—a political party's statement of its general principles and positions on political issues. The parties draw up their platforms during their national conventions.

political party—an organized group that shares a belief in certain political principles and tries to get its members elected to public office.

political patronage—the giving of government jobs or other favors to members of a political party or to those who donate money to the party.

political realignment—a long-term shift of power from one political party to another.

politics—the art and science of government that deals with the form, organization, and management of a state or group of states and their political affairs.

primary elections—elections in which the voters choose a political party's candidates for public office.

prohibition—the nationwide ban on the manufacture and sale of alcoholic beverages under the Eighteenth Amendment. The term also refers to the period during which this amendment was in effect.

prohibitionist—an advocate of the prohibition of the manufacture or sale of alcoholic beverages.

ratification—an official approval of a legal document, such as a constitution.

Reconstruction—the process under which the southern states were reorganized after the Civil War and their relations with the national government were reestablished. The term also refers to the period during which this process took place.

referendum—a process by which citizens of a state vote on a state law, a new state constitution, or an amendment to an existing constitution.

secession—the formal act of withdrawing from an organization, such as a state's decision to leave the United States and form its own government.

sedition—speech or action that incites or causes discontent or rebellion against the government.

tariff—a duty or tax on imported products.

temperance—the use of alcoholic beverages in moderation or abstaining from their use. Some advocates of temperance also support the restriction or prohibition of sales of alcoholic beverages.

ticket—a list of a political party's candidates for public office.

ticket splitting—voting for candidates from more than one political party in a particular election.

trust—a combination of businesses that controls most or all of a particular industry, such as railroads.

veto—the power to reject bills passed by a lawmaking body.

BIBLIOGRAPHY

Aldrich, John H. *Why Parties? The Origin and Transformation of Party Politics in America.* Chicago: University of Chicago Press, 1995.

Binkley, Wilfred A. *American Political Parties: Their Natural History*, 4th ed. New York: Alfred E. Knopf, Inc., 1965.

Brown, Thomas. *Politics and Statesmanship: Essays on the American Whig Party.* New York: Columbia University Press, 1985.

Cunningham, Noble E. *The Presidency of James Monroe.* Lawrence: University of Kansas Press, 1996.

Dangerfield, George. *The Era of Good Feelings.* New York: Harcourt, Brace and Company, 1952. Reprint, Chicago: Ivan R. Dee, Inc., 1989.

Davis, William C. *"A Government of Our Own": The Making of the Confederacy.* New York: The Free Press, 1994.

Ekirch, Arthur A., Jr. *Progressivism in America: A Study of the Era from Theodore Roosevelt to Woodrow Wilson.* New York: New Viewpoints, 1974.

Elkins, Stanley, and Eric McKitrick. *The Age of Federalism: The Early American Republic, 1788–1800.* New York: Oxford University Press, 1997.

Gable, John A. *The Bull Moose Years: Theodore Roosevelt and the Progressive Party.* Port Washington, NY: Kennikat Press, 1978.

Gienapp, William E. *The Origins of the Republican Party, 1852–1856.* New York: Oxford University Press, 1987.

Goodwyn, Lawrence. *The Populist Moment: A Short History of the Agrarian Revolt in America.* New York: Oxford University Press, 1978.

Gordon, John Steele. *Hamilton's Blessing: The Extraordinary Life and Times of Our National Debt.* New York: Walker and Company, 1997.

Hicks, John D. *The Populist Revolt: A History of the Farmers' Alliance and the People's Party.* Minneapolis: University of Minnesota Press, 1931. Reprint, Lincoln: University of Nebraska Press, 1961.

Hofstadter, Richard. *The Age of Reform.* New York: Vintage Books, 1955.

———. *The Idea of a Party System: The Rise of Legitimate Opposition in the United States.* Berkeley: University of California Press, 1969.

Holt, Michael F. *Political Parties and American Political Development from the Age of Jackson to the Age of Lincoln.* Baton Rouge: Louisiana State University Press, 1992.

———. *The Political Crisis of the 1850s.* New York: W. W. Norton & Company, Inc., 1978.

Johnson, Donald Bruce, and Kirk H. Porter, comps. *National Party Platforms 1840–1972.* Urbana: University of Illinois Press, 1973.

Koveter, Peter B., ed. *Democrats and the American Idea: A Bicentennial Appraisal.* Washington, DC: Center for National Policy Press, 1992.

Link, Arthur S., and Richard L. McCormick. *Progressivism.* Arlington Heights, IL: Harlan, Davidson, Inc., 1983.

Main, Jackson Turner. *The Antifederalists: Critics of the Constitution, 1781–1788.* Chapel Hill: University of North Carolina Press, 1961. Reprint, New York: W. W. Norton & Company, Inc., 1974.

McGerr, Michael E. *The Decline of Popular Politics: The American North, 1865–1928.* New York: Oxford University Press, 1986.

Paludan, Phillip Shaw. *The Presidency of Abraham Lincoln.* Lawrence: University of Kansas Press, 1994.

Reichley, A. James. *The Life of the Parties: A History of American Political Parties.* New York: The Free Press, 1992.

Remini, Robert V. *Andrew Jackson,* 3 vols. New York: History Book Club, 1998.

———. *Daniel Webster: The Man and His Time.* New York: W. W. Norton & Company, Inc., 1997.

———. *Henry Clay: Statesman for the Union.* New York: W. W. Norton & Company, Inc., 1991.

———. *Martin Van Buren and the Making of the Democratic Party.* New York: Columbia University Press, 1959.

Schlesinger, Arthur M., Jr. *The Age of Jackson.* Boston: Little, Brown and Company, 1945.

Wattenberg, Martin P. *The Decline of American Political Parties, 1952–1988.* Cambridge: Harvard University Press, 1990.

Wilson, Major L. *The Presidency of Martin Van Buren.* Lawrence: University of Kansas Press, 1984.

Page numbers in *italics* refer to illustrations.